100 Ideas for Drama

Gordon Lamont
Steve Ball
Betsy Blatchley
John Goodwin
Duncan Greig

English

PSHE

History

RE

Geography

Science

Art

PE

Maths

Gordon Lamont (compiler) is a Chief Producer with BBC Education and works regularly with teachers in primary schools, advocating the value of drama across the curriculum.

Steve Ball is the founder and director of two Theatre in Education companies and has a wealth of experience of drama in schools.

Betsy Blatchley has worked extensively in educational drama and is currently producer – mobile tours for the Royal National Theatre Education Department.

John Goodwin is a senior lecturer at the University of Portsmouth where his responsibilities include tutoring courses for teachers.

Duncan Greig is a deputy headteacher at a primary school where he encourages the use of drama in cross-curricular links.

Collins Educational
An imprint of HarperCollins*Publishers*

Published by Collins Educational
An imprint of HarperCollins*Publishers*
77–85 Fulham Palace Road
Hammersmith
London
W6 8JB

First published 1997

ISBN 0 00 312012 0

Editor: Mitzi Bales

Illustrations: Bethan Matthews

Cover design: Clive Wilson

Cover photograph: Martin Soukias

Text page design: The Design Works, Reading

Printed and bound: Martins the Printers Ltd, Berwick on Tweed

The author and publisher would like to thank the staff and children of Larkrise First School, Oxford where the cover photograph was taken.

Contents

Introduction

Introduction

Our aim in this book is to present clear, accessible ideas for primary drama. These 100 ideas have been designed to enrich topic work and feed into a range of curriculum subjects. All the authors encourage you to adapt the ideas to your own teaching style and curriculum needs. Drama is a powerful teaching tool. We hope that this book widens its use across the curriculum and across the country.

How do the ideas link with the curriculum?

Almost every part of the curriculum can be enhanced by applying the AS IF of drama to its teaching. In drama, children can freely try out situations and actions, empathise with others and enter into imaginary worlds. The traditional strongholds of drama, English and PSHE, are well served in the book, with many ideas exploring old and new stories, ethical dilemmas and social situations. These in particular help to develop speaking and listening skills. There are History ideas using drama to gain insights into times past such as the lives of the Victorians. Drama allows us to deal with Victorian servants AS IF it is our first nervous day at the Big House or AS IF we are children down the mines, up the chimneys or in the factories. You will find ideas linked to Science, one of which, for example, looks at issues related to energy and the environment. Other ideas are linked to Geography, Maths, Art, RE and PE. To help you find your way around, the ideas are organised under the broad headings of English, PSHE, History and Other Subjects. The last heading is broken down into the individual subjects they treat.

What skills will you need?

Using drama in the classroom requires only the skills and abilities you already employ everyday in management, storytelling and drawing the best out of each child. However, there are a number of strategies that are common to drama and that help you draw on your skills. We have emboldened the first use of these strategies in each idea to signal that they are in the glossary in case you are not familiar with them.

Designed for ease of use

Each idea provides a quick reference in the margin so that you can easily choose an activity appropriate for your class. First, an icon identifies the subject. (Some ideas have more than one icon, reflecting the cross-curricular strengths of drama.) Then comes an indication of the age range. (This can only be a suggestion, as many ideas can be applied across a wider age range, perhaps with small adaptations.) Next either the hall or the classroom is suggested as the space to use. (You may find that you can use less space with a small adaptation to the idea.) Following is a breakdown of the groupings required, in the order they occur. (These comprise small groups, pairs, whole class, individuals and groups of a specific number.) If resources or background work are necessary, these are also indicated. Then comes any accompanying photocopiable master (pcm) crucial to the activities. The pcm is further cross referenced in the text. The Contents pages have also been designed to help you quickly and easily find an idea suitable for your class.

Enriching your school's programme

Going to the theatre or inviting a children's theatre group to your school not only can inspire further work of a focused nature, but can also encourage an interest in drama and the arts in general. There are a number of well established professional children's theatre companies that tour schools with plays ranging from fairy stories to serious, issue-based dramas. Theatre in Education (TIE) gives children the opportunity to work with professional actors who have devised material especially for the curriculum. Your local Education Authority can advise you of any groups in your area, and local theatres might also be helpful.

Glossary

Brainstorming
In a group, freely offering ideas, solutions and questions on a given subject or problem, without comment, criticism or discussion. Often the contributions are listed and then explored in more detail later.

Bring or come to life
Calling for the participants in a still picture to move into actions, and sometimes speech, consistent with that picture.

Caption
A title or heading that accompanies another piece of work, such as a still picture. It describes or comments on the action.

Character or role
A person, or sometimes an animal, represented in a play or film by an actor and in a book by description. In the context of this book, it also means representing someone or something in a role play or still picture.

Conscience alley
A strategy allowing pro and con arguments to be considered by a character in role, who walks between two rows of children (the alley). Each side offers alternative warnings and advice, representing the conscience of the character. At the end of the rows, the character must make a decision based on which side was more convincing.

Discuss
This term is used in this book to mean an exchange of ideas involving the whole class and the teacher.

Forum theatre
A situation is enacted by children assigned the established roles as the rest of the class watches. At any point, and with the teacher mediating, those watching can stop the action to discuss and suggest different responses to the roles, and new developments in the situation. Other children take on any new roles as appropriate.

Freeze
Stopping all action and sound as if on a video freeze frame or like a still photograph capturing a moment in time.

Hot seat
A chair or place to sit where a character in role is put on the spot with questions about behaviour, attitudes, plans and so on. The character answers in role and the questioners may be in or out of role.

Improvisation
Trying out an idea or situation in drama, working in pairs, small groups or as a whole class. Improvisation may be spontaneous as a situation arises, or planned before presenting a scene.

In role
Imagining being someone else in a drama and showing how that character might behave.

Meeting
Gathering together in role to discuss an issue, solve a problem or plan and agree a course of action.

Mime
Using bodily movement and gestures, without words, to express an idea, show an action or portray a character.

Mind picture
Imagining an event or place in the mind to set a scene or move action forwards. This works best with the eyes closed and can be accompanied by narration, music or sound.

Modelling
Moving a body into a position appropriate to the character or action of a drama.

Movement sequence
Using a series of movements, improvised or rehearsed, to explore a situation, place, feeling or event. Movement sequences can be more abstract than mime.

Narrate
To tell a story or part of a story to set the scene, offer information or move the drama on in time. The children either listen to the narration or enact it as it is spoken. There are times when children might narrate.

Out of role
Stepping out of the drama to become yourself again.

Prop
A moveable object used in drama.

Ritual
Agreed and rehearsed movement, sound or word, or a combination of these, usually with a sense of solemnity, used to mark signficant moments in a drama or to begin and end it.

Role
see Character or role

Role play
1 (verb) To act the part of a character in a scene.
2 (noun) A situation to be enacted.

Scene
An incident or situation in a drama. A scene can be improvised or refined and rehearsed to be presented as a piece of theatre.

Signal
Any prearranged sign, for example, a hand clap, a whistle, standing with arms akimbo, used to start or end the action of a drama or within a drama; to indicate speakers in thought tracking; or on other occasions when simple communication is needed.

Sound collage or montage
The representation of a place, mood, theme or story in sound. Instruments, the voice or objects of many kinds can be used.

Still picture
Using the body, individually or in groups, to create a composition that remains frozen once composed. It can represent a slice of time, like a photograph, or be more abstract and thematic, like a painting or sculpture.

Solo movement
A child moving on her or his own within the context of the drama.

Thought tracking
Children speaking aloud what they think characters, either their own or others, would be thinking at a given point in the drama. This is often used during or after a still picture to explore meanings and emotions.

1 Giant's footprint

Drama space
Hall

Organisation
Whole class

Resources
A length of rope or piece of chalk

Age
5–7

Purpose
● To provide motivation for speaking, writing and listening within a lively drama context.

Activities
1 Ask the class to make up an original name for a fictional country and agree it.

2 Outline a giant footprint on the hall floor, using rope or chalk. (You may wish to draw round children lying down as the giant's toes.) Ask the class about the shape you have created. *What might the giant look like? What kind of creature is the giant? Why is the footprint near the village?* After a few answers, say that the action of the drama might offer more and clearer answers.

3 Create a **still picture** around the footprint with each member of the class **in role** as a villager. Take time to build the still picture with each child stepping carefully and slowly into it upon your **signal**. Try to work in silence, building up an atmosphere of strangeness and uncertainty.

4 Ask the class to relax in position and to think about what would be going through the minds of the villagers as they discover the footprint for the first time. Each child should then choose a word or phrase to express the thought, such as, *I'm really scared*; *terror*; *It's so huge*, etc. Then re-form the still picture and move round the group tapping each child on the shoulder as a signal to express their thoughts aloud in turn (**thought tracking**).

5 Arrange a **meeting** in the village to decide what is to be done next, with you in role as the chief of the village. Try to devise means of communicating with the giant. You might need special giant language or very big writing.

6 Send a friendly message to the giant. Come out of the drama. In small groups, ask the children to make still pictures, and/or tell stories, showing what happens next.

2 Who am I?

Drama space
Classroom

Organisation
Whole class

Age
5–7

Purpose
● To encourage thoughtful, structured questions.

Activities
1 Explain that you are going to pretend to be someone the class has heard about recently, but you are not going to say who. Choose a familiar fictional or historical character such as Bo Peep, Robin Hood, Anansi, Mrs Butler, Hanuman.

2 Sit on your **special chair** and invite the children to ask you questions about who you are. If necessary, stand up and, **out of role**, suggest the kind of questions the children might ask: *Are you an animal? Are you from a book? Are you a nice or a nasty character?*

3 Continue until the children guess the character. Older children might have a go in the hot seat themselves.

3 Storytelling

Drama space
Classroom

Organisation
Whole class

Resources
Tape recorder, cassette

Age
5–7

Purpose
● To develop basic storytelling skills.

Activities
1 Sit in a circle. Begin telling a simple, original story and continue only until you spark the children's imaginations (see right for some ideas).
2 Ask each child to add a line or two. Encourage them to make the story as wild and weird as they wish.
3 Do this a couple of times more with different story lines.
4 Once the children have gained in confidence, tape record a story and play it back for the class to enjoy.

Some suggestions for beginnings of stories:

1 Once there was a very wicked king who was cruel to his people and made them work very hard. The people were sad and wished they could have a new king. One day a stranger arrived in town and asked…

2 Sangeeta woke up feeling excited. She couldn't think why and then she remembered it was her birthday. She jumped out of bed and ran downstairs. She expected to find lots of presents in the kitchen but…

3 In a farm deep in the country there lived a very clever pig and a very mischievous mouse. They were great friends but the mouse was always getting the pig into trouble. One day the farmer brought the pig's food as usual. The mouse said to the pig, 'Why do you eat that horrible stuff. I know where you could get some better food'. The mouse then suggested…

4 The three wishes

Drama space
Classroom or hall

Organisation
Whole class, groups of 3

Resources
A wand or other symbol of magic

Age
5–7

Purposes
● To begin to work creatively in groups.
● To follow simple instructions.
● To respond to teacher **in role**.

Activities
1 Take on the role of a magician. Pick up the magic wand and encourage the children to ask you questions about your life, your spells and the kind of magic you do. Try to build up an air of mystery and fun.
2 **Out of role**, ask the children to **mime** getting out of bed, getting dressed and having breakfast. Explain to them that when the magician waves the magic wand and calls out **freeze,** everyone should remain exactly in place and completely still.

3 Return to the role and, once the children are miming, freeze the action. Announce that they are going to be granted three wishes.
4 Out of role, ask the children to get into groups of three. Ask each group to decide on three wishes.
5 In role, visit each group to find out their three wishes.
6 Ask each group to choose one of the wishes and act out a short **scene** which shows what would happen if their wish came true. Come out of the drama. The scenes, or parts of them, can be performed for the rest of the class.

5 Nursery rhymes

Drama space
Classroom or hall

Organisation
Whole class, small groups

Background
Practice in speaking
nursery rhymes together

Age
5–7

Purposes
● To develop storytelling and movement skills.
● To encourage the use of imagination in drama.

Activities
1 Read or sing one of the nursery rhymes below.
2 Ask the children to describe the pictures they see in their mind for each line (**mind picture**). Encourage them to use their imaginations rather than remembering what they have seen in books.
3 Discuss each piece of action in the rhyme and talk to the children about how they could enact that activity. Ask: *How do you create the wall for Humpty Dumpty? How do you show that Humpty Dumpty is in pieces?* Work with a few children for each activity while the others watch.
4 Split the children into groups of about four. Give each group a line or part of a line to **mime.** Encourage them to create everything without **props**. For example, two children could be a tuffet, one child could be a bowl, another a spoon. If your class is large, you might choose to work with two nursery rhymes.
5 Explain that you will be the storyteller. Sit the groups in order of the lines around the room. Say each line or part of a line slowly and then point to the appropriate group to perform their mime. Come out of the drama. For younger children, you could tape the narration so that you can oversee the performance more closely.

Further activities
▶ After a few rehearsals, the piece could be performed for another class or for parents.

/ indicates possible division into sections for mime

Little Miss Muffet
Sat on her tuffet/
Eating her curds and whey/
There came a big spider
Who sat down beside her/
And frightened Miss Muffet away/

Humpty Dumpty sat on a wall/
Humpty Dumpty had a great fall/
All the king's horses
And all the king's men/
Couldn't put Humpty together again/

Three blind mice, three blind mice/
See how they run, see how they run/
They all ran after the farmer's wife/
Who cut off their tails with a carving knife/
Did you ever see such a thing in your life
As three blind mice/

This final nursery rhyme could be used for older children. Encourage them to include more detail.

Sing a song of sixpence, a pocket full of rye/
Four and twenty blackbirds baked in a pie/
When the pie was opened the birds began to sing/
Wasn't that a dainty dish to set before the king/
The king was in his counting house counting out his money/
The queen was in the parlour eating bread and honey/
The maid was in the garden hanging out the clothes/
When down came a blackbird and pecked off her nose/
She made such a commotion that little Jenny Wren
Flew down into the garden and pecked it on again/

6 Jack and the beanstalk

Drama space
Hall

Organisation
Pairs, groups

Background
Familiarity with the story

Age
5–7

Purpose
● To explore a popular story through drama.

Activities

1 Working in pairs, one child pretends to be Jack and the other his mother. Say that Jack has just returned with a handful of beans instead of money for the cow. Ask: *What might his mother say?* (Remind the children that the cow was their last possession.) What might Jack say to try to persuade his mother that he made a good bargain?

2 Standing in a circle, the children imagine they can see the amazing plant stretching high into the sky. Ask them about how they feel, what they see and what they think they should do next.

3 Working in a space of their own, the children imagine they are climbing up the beanstalk. It is very hard going. The branches are bendy and nearly out of reach so that they have to stretch precariously as they climb.

4 They find themselves outside a huge castle with an enormous door. In pairs, **out of role**, they decide how they might introduce themselves to whoever lives in the castle.

5 Narrate a **movement sequence** in which they decide to sneak into the castle first to have a look round. They push open the very heavy door and move into the castle. They move cautiously about the castle, feeling tiny where everything is so huge. Then they meet the giant's wife in the corridor and introduce themselves in the way they had decided.

6 You take the role of the giant's wife and warn them that the giant likes to eat small children as a snack. You may also tell them about the giant's treasures: two big sacks of gold; a chicken that lays golden eggs; and a golden harp that sings.

7 Working in groups, each group decides which of the giant's treasures to steal and then creates a **still picture** of the theft. They will need to think about what each person in the group is doing, and how to express the tension of this nerve-wracking moment.

8 The children sit in a circle to discuss whether Jack was right to take the giant's belongings. What do they think about the way Jack behaved?

 # 7 Magic beans

Drama space
Hall

Organisation
Solo, pairs

Resources
Any version of *Jack and the Beanstalk*

Age
5–7

Purposes
● To use the story of Jack and the beanstalk as the starting point for imaginative storytelling and drama.
● To encourage the whole class to work together.

Activities

1 Tell or read the story of Jack and the beanstalk and discuss it with the children so that they become familiar with the sequence of events at the start of the story.

2 Do some simple **solo movement** depicting the start of the story. **Narrate** the sequence as the children enact it:
– Jack waking and setting off for the market, leading the cow
– walking down the lane
– crossing the river on stepping stones (still leading the cow)
– stopping for a picnic lunch
– setting off again, becoming more tired
– stopping for a rest

3 Working in pairs, they pick up the story and enact the selling of the cow for five magic beans. Encourage them to haggle and strike a bargain rather than agreeing at once. (Stop the action after a while to watch some children's enactment.)

4 Narrate: 'Jack takes the beans home and his mother throws them out of the window in anger. He goes to sleep and the next morning looks out of the window.' Now ask each pair to create their own version of the story from this point onwards. Encourage them to come up with a different idea: *Do the beans grow so huge that Jack and his mother can live inside them? Do they grow such thick foliage that the two are trapped inside the house? Do they grow into a giant bridge across the sea to Canada or across the sky to the moon?* Call the whole class together and have each pair tell their story.

8 The rhyme machine

Drama space
Hall

Organisation
Whole class, pairs

Resources
A small drum

Age
5–7

pcm 8A on page 60

pcm 8B on page 61

Purpose
● To provide children with opportunities to experiment with language, especially rhymes.

Activities

1 Provide sufficient copies of pcm 8A for each child and ask the class to imagine that the hall is a very old scrap yard. Ask them to search the area for scattered pieces of old machinery like those in the pcm. The pieces may be very heavy and will need careful handling and lifting. Indicate a place in the hall where the pieces should be placed, and ask them to **mime** lifting, carrying and placing the scrap.

2 Examine the imaginary pieces and ask the children to guess the possible purpose of the machine. *Why all these cogs? gears? pulleys, etc?* After a few guesses, say that it is a rhyme machine.

3 Ask some of the children to assemble the parts to make one big machine in the middle of the space.

4 **Narrate solo movements**. Say the following:
'Make your body into metal. You have stiff arms, hands and legs and are part of a machine that is very stiff and still. Now the machine is getting ready to move. (Beat a drum.) The machine is slowly moving and each part is getting into action. Move your body to the beat of the drum. Remember, you are made of metal.'

5 In pairs, children watch each other and join their movements together wherever they can. You may need to help in this. Then place all the pairs to assemble the most interesting looking machine possible. **Freeze** action.

6 Remind the children that this is a rhyme machine and will need their rhymes to be able to operate. Unfreeze the action. Produce one of the tapes (see pcm 8B) and work with the children to make up rhymes for the word on it. Write the rhymes on the tape. Then re-create the machine and bring it to life by chanting the words on the ticker tape. As the words are spoken, the children move the ticker tape through the machine, passing it from one to another with mechanical movements.

9 In the attic

Drama space
Hall

Organisation
Solo, pairs

Age
5–7

Purpose
● To stimulate the imagination by taking a make-believe journey.

Activities

1 The children **mime** climbing a narrow ladder into a dark attic. Once there they move around very carefully so that they don't bump into anything or hurt themselves. Encourage a sense of tense, careful movement.

2 **Narrate** briefly a story which involves finding a window and pulling back a lacy curtain. Light streams in. The children sit down and close their eyes. Ask them to think about what they can see in the attic. Ask a few children to describe what they see.

3 Tell them that in one corner is a large wooden chest inside of which are lots of different uniforms and costumes. Working with a partner, ask the children to mime putting on one of the outfits and showing the rest of the class how they move in it. The class attempts to guess the costume.

10 The enormous turnip

Drama space
Hall

Organisation
Solo, pairs, small groups, whole class

Background
Familiarity with the story

Age
5–7

Purpose
- To use drama to explore this traditional tale.

Activities

1 The children imagine and **mime** being farmers in a field. First they prepare the ground for planting, so some dig, others hoe. Then they plant turnip seeds.

2 One turnip is beginning to grow bigger and bigger and bigger. In pairs, ask the children to express their amazement in a simple sentence. Encourage the use of descriptive language both of the turnip and their reaction to it.

3 In small groups, they try to pull the turnip out of the ground. (Remind them that it is difficult to get a grip on a turnip.) The turnip just won't budge. Encourage mime that shows the strain and effort of trying to pull out the turnip. Finally, they succeed. You could end this part of the activities with three **still pictures** created consecutively:

It's stuck!
It's moving!
It's out!

4 The children sit in a circle. The turnip is going to be made into a stew. Ask each child to add something good to the stew.

5 In small groups, ask the children to think of who else they would like to invite to an Enormous Turnip Stew Party. Then enact the party.

11 The old woman in the shoe

Drama space
Hall

Subject link
PSHE

Organisation
Whole class, pairs

Resources
A length of material;
skipping ropes, chairs

Age
5–7

Purpose
- To explore the well-known nursery rhyme in a new way.

Activities

1 Read the rhyme to the children (see below). Discuss its meaning and list questions the children might have. Explain that some of the questions will probably be answered through the drama they are going to do.

> There was an old woman
> who lived in a shoe.
> She had so many children
> she didn't know what to do.
> She gave them some soup
> without any bread,
> Then whipped them all soundly
> and sent them to bed.

2 Using a clear space, let the class create the shoe house with simple objects such as: a length of material for the tongue of the shoe house; a couple of chairs for the doorway; a skipping rope for a washing line. When the shoe house is completed, ask the class to stand away from it and choose someone to describe the inside of the shoe house as they imagine it to be. *What does it look like? How big is it? How many rooms are there? What would it be like to live in a shoe house like this?*

3 Ask the children to pretend they live in the shoe. They might be doing jobs around the house, or gardening, or playing games and so on. Working in pairs, the children create a **still picture** when they have decided what each is doing.

4 Take the **hot seat in role** as the old woman. Emphasise how poor you are and answer the children's questions about a life of poverty. Set up meal time, with very hungry children waiting in a long queue holding a soup bowl. Have them **mime** devouring every tiny drop of soup. Mime that there is not enough soup to go around.

5 In pairs, the children try to think of ways of making life better. In turn, each child explains their ideas to the old woman.

12 Explorers

Drama space
Hall

Organisation
Whole class

Age
5–7

Purpose
- To use movement as the stimulus for an imaginative story.

Activities

1 Ask the children to find a space and to lie down on their backs. Build up a mind picture of an imaginary jungle. Describe the heat, the sounds, the shape of the plants and the different animals.

2 As you build the picture, ask the children to stand and use their bodies to create the shapes you mention.

3 Create a **sound montage** of the jungle, bringing different sounds in and out as you conduct.

4 Now ask the class to imagine they have just burst into a clearing and see the

ruins of a large city. Working in groups, ask them to create a **still picture** showing the moment of discovery.

5 Ask the children to think about what they should do next. They have made this amazing discovery and have set up camp just on the edge of the city. How should they proceed? Discuss and try to reach a consensus. During the discussion, adopt a sceptical role: you are for abandoning the quest as too dangerous, for example.

6 In groups, the children create **mimes**, short **scenes** or still pictures based on the decision in step 5. Ask them to decide on either a happy or sad ending.

13 The selfish giant

Drama space
Hall

 Subject link
PSHE

Organisation
Pairs, groups, fours, whole class

Background
Familiarity with the story

Age
5–9

Purposes
- To provide a new perspective on a classic children's story.
- To allow children to explore PSHE issues.

Activities

1 In groups, the children enter the giant's garden. As you tap their shoulder one at a time, they describe what they see. They then start to **mime** playing games.

2 In groups, ask the children to create a **still picture** showing their reaction to seeing the giant. Encourage them to think about how to indicate where the giant is and his size. Ask them to think of words that describe their feelings.

3 In fours as Snow, Frost, Hail and North

Wind, the children move around the giant's garden. Snow is 'spreading a long white cloak', Hail 'dancing on the roof and cracking the slates', North wind 'roaring all day and blowing off the chimney pots', Frost 'painting all the trees silver'.

4 The winter has come and the giant is all alone in his castle. Discuss what the giant may be doing and feeling. Take the role of the giant and let the children ask why you threw them out of the garden.

5 The wall has been knocked down and the children have been welcomed into the garden. The children create a still picture of their entry back into the garden, then you **bring** it **to life**.

6 The giant has died. How will the children remember him?

14 The drought of Chi-Min-Tin

Drama space
Classroom or hall

Subject link
RE

Organisation
Whole class, pairs, groups

Resources
Masks; tape recorder and percussion instruments would be useful

Age
7–9

pcm 14 on page 62

Purpose

● To provide opportunities for speaking, listening and reading, stimulated by a legend from another culture.

Activities

1 Provide sufficient copies of pcm 14 for all the children. Read the text and discuss the images or moments which make the greatest impact upon the class. Experiment with speaking parts of the text aloud. Use a whole-class chorus, individual voices, pairs and small groups to provide contrast. Try to capture the rhythm of the piece, but don't spend too long at it. You may wish to tape record a successful version.

2 The story does not say what happens when Mi-Lin and her companion went into the Jagyard mountains. In pairs, the children talk over what they think might have happened on the journey, considering each of the three days individually.

3 Enlarge the pairs into groups of four. Each group agrees on a version of the journey and acts it out. You might want to provide masks and percussion

instruments. Suggest that the groups use the techniques of **freezing** the action at key moments; **miming** climbing; and **narrating**.

Further activities

► Present the whole story as a drama performance in an assembly or to an invited audience.

15 Iron man

Drama space
Hall

Organisation
Small groups, whole class, pairs

Background
Familiarity with *The Iron Man* by Ted Hughes

Age
7–11

Purpose

● To express reactions to this well-known book.

Activities

1 In small groups, the children **mime** trying to help rebuild the Iron Man. Remind them that parts of him will be very heavy and will need more than one person to move; some are delicate and need careful handling; others will require a search as they have been scattered all over the beach.

2 Everyone stands in a big group. They are near the edge of a cliff. Up over the edge of the cliff comes the Iron Man. What does he look like? How do they feel on seeing such a huge figure? Move round asking each child for words or phrases to describe what they see and what they feel.

3 In small groups, the children try to decide what should be done with the Iron Man. Remind them that many people are very frightened of him.

4 Everyone forms a big circle. Tell them they are on the edge of the pit into which the Iron Man has fallen. Quickly move round the group finding out what each child feels about trapping the Iron Man.

Further activities

► In groups of four, the children think up a menu for the Iron Man, perhaps a starter of lightly greased springs, followed by half a truck and a pudding of brass ball bearings.

► In pairs, the children try to think of arguments to persuade the Iron Man to fight the Space-Bat-Angel-Dragon.

► In a large circle, the children try to think how they would thank the Iron Man.

16 The snow queen

Drama space
Hall

Organisation
Pairs, groups, whole class

Background
Familiarity with the story

Age
7–9

Purpose
● To encourage responses to literature.

Activities
1 In pairs, the children imagine the ground is covered with snow and that they have been allowed out to play in it for the first time this year. They play all sorts of games. Remind them that it is bitterly cold.

2 In small groups, they create a **still picture** showing the Snow Queen and the people in the town. Ask them to make the picture express what they are thinking and feeling. Are they worried? frightened? excited? interested?

3 In the old woman's house, formed by the children in a circle, ask one of the children to stand in the middle. The others try to persuade her or him to stay with the old woman. They can use ideas from the story or make up their reasons.

4 Ask the children to think of the most beautiful things they can imagine. Then ask each child to move to a given space and, as they describe their object, add it to an imaginary pile. Slowly build up the collection of beautiful things.

5 In pairs, one child is the Gerda figure, one is a robber who has taken her prisoner. Gerda tries to persuade the robber not to hurt her, even to let her go. Tell them the robber has a kind heart. What can Gerda say that would make the robber let her go? Allow the drama to go on for a few minutes.

6 Set the **scene** in the Snow Queen's palace by building a still picture of all the children as frozen statues. **In role** as the queen, move round **modelling** some of the children's positions or shapes. Then **freeze** the still picture. Say you are changing your role to become Gerda. Search for your brother. When you find him, the statues **mime** how they begin to defrost and finally become unfrozen. Each child comes to you, introduces themselves and thanks you for freeing them.

17 Rescue

Drama space
Classroom or hall

  Subject link
Geography

Organisation
Groups

Resources
A bottle with the message (right) in it

Age
7–11

Purposes
● To create a story from a stimulus and develop speaking and listening skills.
● To focus on communication.

Activities
1 Tell the children that you are going to do a drama about a message in a bottle. Show the class the bottle with the message in it.

> **A hand-written note on weathered paper which says:**
>
> Please help. We are stranded. 40 degrees north; 20 degrees west.
>
> Our boat is sinking. Send help immediately.

2 In groups, the children decide who they think the message is from and in what circumstances it was sent. (For example, people who are lost or have been shipwrecked.) Each group devises and **mimes** a short **scene** which begins with something going wrong and finishes with the bottle with the message being thrown into the water. See a few scenes and then explain that the message leads to a rescue.

3 Create a photograph of the rescue by means of a **still image**.

4 Set up a press conference in the drama space. Divide the class into a group which has been rescued and a group which are television, radio and newspaper reporters. Those rescued answer reporters' questions.

18 Creating characters

Drama space
Classroom

Organisation
Individuals, whole class

Resources
Blackboard or flip chart

Age
7–9

Purposes
● To develop movement skills.
● To create characters through movement.

Activities
1 Sitting in a circle, ask for one child to volunteer to be the model and two others to volunteer to be the modellers. Explain that they are going to lead the class in a game, and ask the model to stand in the middle of the circle.

2 Ask the modellers to stand to one side and choose a **character** from a book or a film, without letting anyone hear the name. The rest of the group watch as the modellers move the model's body and face gently to create the character. (For example, Mrs Butler, Robin Hood.)

3 Encourage the model to hold the pose while the rest of the class try to guess the character. List all the ideas on the backboard or flip chart. The modellers then say who the character is.

4 Now split the class into groups of three and ask each group to organise themselves as two modellers and a model. They then choose one of the characters listed in step 3 and transform their model into that character. Share all the characters with the rest of the class.

5 Ask the two modellers in each group to take the same pose as their model. Explain that the characters are now going to **come to life**.

6 Talk the children through a series of simple activities, such as making a drink, cleaning their teeth, eating a sandwich, and ask them to enact the actions as they feel their character would.

19 Robin Hood

Drama space
Classroom or hall

Organisation
Whole class

Resources
Tables and chairs

Background
Familiarity with the Robin Hood legend

Age
7–11

pcm 19 on page 63

Purposes
● To work together on a scripted drama, **bringing** it **to life** from the page.
● To provide a stimulus for further playwriting.

Activities
1 Read the **scene** on pcm 19 together and discuss the story line.

2 Create the market with tables and chairs for the market stalls and the archery target. Ask the children to choose a **role** from among buyer, seller, entertainer, soldier. Allow time to prepare and rehearse these roles. Suggest that entertainers might be jugglers or singers or players of an instrument. Ask buyers to adopt family roles such as mother and father and work out what they should buy. Remind soldiers to set up the archery target. Encourage each child to think about character and actions.

3 Bring the market scene to life for a few minutes, then stop and give suggestions for how it can be improved. Try to make it lead naturally into the script.

4 Now add the scripted part after filling the roles of Robin and the Sheriff with volunteers. Be sure there are three soldiers. Work on the delivery of the words by the principals and the reactions of the onlookers to what is going on.

5 Discuss why Robin enters the archery contest. Do the children think he wishes to be arrested and taken into the castle? If he has set this up deliberately, why?

Further activity
▶ In pairs or individually, ask the children to write the next scene of the play as they imagine it will happen.

20 Magic journeys

Drama space
Classroom

Organisation
Groups of 3 or 4 , then two groups

Resources
Pens or pencils; musical instruments; tape recorder and cassette; story outline on board in advance

Age
7–9

Note
You will only need enough copies of the pcm to be shared among the groups

pcm 20 on page 64

Purpose
● To encourage creative writing skills and develop these into scriptwriting.

Activities
1 Split the children into groups of three or four and give each group a copy of pcm 20.
2 Depending on the ability of the children, either read the pcm to them or ask them to read it as a group. Ask each group to fill in the spaces in the most imaginative ways they can think of. You may wish to discuss some possibilities as a whole class to encourage them to think imaginatively and creatively.

3 Ask a representative from each group to read their story to the class.
4 As a class decide on the most exciting or outlandish ideas from all the versions you have heard. Fill the spaces in the outline story on the blackboard with these.
5 Split the class into two groups and ask each group to create noises and sound effects for one section of the story. They could use their voices, objects in the classroom and/or musical instruments.
6 Present a radio drama by taping the story with actors and sound effects.

21 Lost property

Drama space
Classroom or hall

Organisation
Whole class, small groups

Resources
Selection of objects both ordinary (such as pen, watch, wallet) and extraordinary (such as a mousetrap, sink plug, false teeth)

Age
7–9

Purpose
● To encourage problem solving.

Activities
1 **In role** as a police officer in charge of lost property at the local police station. Talk about your job and the variety of weird and wonderful things that people lose, such as false teeth, large statues, a bird cage.
2 **Out of role**, show the class the objects that were recently handed in.

3 Split the class into small groups and give each group an object. Ask them to decide who they think lost the object and how it might have been lost.
4 Ask each group to create a **still picture** of the owner with the object before it was lost.
5 Ask each group to use this still picture as a starting point for a short **scene** either showing how the objects were lost or what happens when the owner arrives at the lost property office.

22 Before and after

Drama space
Classroom or hall

Organisation
Whole class, small groups

Age
7–9

Purposes
● To serve as an ice breaker for a new class unused to working together.
● To encourage co-operation as well as having fun together.

Activities
1 Discuss the idea of photographs being taken before and after an event. Describe the following and see if the class can guess what happens in between.
– *Before:* a mighty ocean liner sets sail with cheering crowds.
  After: a wreath floats on the water.
– *Before:* a boy rubs his stomach with a hungry gleam in his eye. In front of him is a table piled high with delicious food.
  After: The boy is in bed holding his stomach and turns his nose up at an offered chocolate.
– *Before:* a girl stands nonchalantly in front of a lion's cage.
  After: the lion chews happily on a bone.

2 In small groups, the children make their own sets of before and after photographs as **still images**. Encourage careful thought and co-operation in planning. Remind them that the before and after pictures have to give a clue to the missing middle one. Share the pictures with the whole class who have to guess what happened between the pictures.

Further activity
▶ Talk together about advertisements which use the before and after technique, for example, slimming adverts. In the same groups, the children invent a new wonder product such as an instant smartness pill. They then work out a before and after advertisement for TV or radio. Remind them of the importance of clarity and brevity, and encourage each group to think up a name for the wonder product and a simple slogan or jingle to use in the advert.

23 Dracula's castle

Drama space
Classroom

Organisation
Individuals, pairs, whole class

Resources
Tape recorder

Age
9–11

pcm 23 on page 65

Purposes
● To provide an opportunity for speaking and writing in response to a printed text.
● To raise awareness of the classics of popular fiction.

Activities
1 Read the text on pcm 23 aloud together, asking individuals and pairs to read lines to add variety and encourage participation. The coachman's lines might be spoken by the whole class. Aim to create a mood of gloom and menace.
2 Create a whole-class **sound collage** of the **scene**. Sounds could include the wind

in the trees, coach wheels, horses neighing, wolves baying. Build these as a collage with one sound overlapping the next, and sounds approaching and receding as appropriate. Orchestrate the sounds to vary volume, tone and pace. Tape record the sound collage.
3 Reread the printed text, this time assigning lines to individuals, pairs, groups and the whole class. Add the sound collage to the reading.

Further activities
▶ Rehearse and perform in an assembly or for other classes.

24 Holding the baby

Drama space
Classroom or hall

Subject link
PSHE

Organisation
Whole class, pairs

Age
9–11

pcm 24 on page 66

Purpose
● To gain an understanding of parenting.

Activities

1 Look at pcm 24 together. Explain that the text is an extract from the opening scene of a TV play. The **characters** are Karen and Jim, a married couple, and their twin babies. Read the extract a few times with different children taking the roles. Play around with the words, encouraging a lively, naturalistic **scene**. Point out that the directions in a TV script are just as important as the spoken dialogue. Discuss the extract, asking: Why is Jim so nervous about looking after the twins? How would you describe his character? How would you describe Karen? What does this short extract indicate about them and their marriage?

2 **Hot seat** the characters. As individuals take on the role of Karen or Jim, they answer the questions from step 1 and any others the children think of.

3 In pairs, the children think about how the scene might develop and share their ideas with the rest of the class.

4 The pairs choose a scene from the play and enact it.

5 Some of the pairs perform their scenes while you list the questions and issues they raise about parenting. Hold a class discussion on the subject.

25 Emma is missing

Drama space
Classroom or hall

Subject link
PSHE

Organisation
Whole class, small groups, individuals

Resources
A collection of objects which might belong to a 12-year-old girl

Age
9–11

Purpose
● To stimulate a range of writing with real audiences in mind.
● To explore the dilemma of a 12-year-old girl.

Activities

1 **In role** as a plain clothes police officer, perhaps putting on a jacket as a costume, say that 12-year-old Emma has gone missing. Use another name if there is an Emma in the class. She was last seen at 5 pm yesterday at the local supermarket where she occasionally worked stacking shelves. ('Erm. Humph. That's illegal at her age, you know.') Produce a bag of her belongings, which you say was found in a supermarket trolley and dumped in the car park. Pass around the objects and ask questions of the class: Do they know her? Has anyone seen her in the last 24 hours?

2 **Out of role**, ask the class who they would like to interview about Emma: parents, friends, supermarket manager. Ask for volunteers to take these roles and hot seat them in turn.

3 Move the story on by explaining that a short handwritten letter from Emma has just been pushed through her parent's letterbox. Ask each child to write this letter; then in role you read some of them to the class.

4 Individually or in small groups, the children write about the case so far in one of the following styles: an official report by the police officer; a story for the local newspaper; a report for local TV or radio.

5 In small groups, the children write or improvise a short **scene** showing how the story ends: happy? sad? unresolved? The same groups enact their scenes for the rest of the class.

26 A midsummer night's dream

Drama space
Classroom or hall

 Subject link
History

Organisation
6 groups

Age
9–11

Note
You will need one whole copy of the pcm and one copy cut into the three sections.

 pcm 26 on page 67

Purpose
● To introduce Shakespeare's language and characters.

Activities
1 Explain that Puck is a very mischievous creature, a servant of Oberon, the King of the Fairies. Puck loves playing tricks on people. In the speech you are going to read, he describes three tricks he has played. Read the speech all the way through.

2 Reread each of the three sections of the speech slowly and see if the children can work out what the trick is in each section: Confusing a fat old horse by pretending to be its foal; turning himself into a crab and getting into a woman's cup, scaring her into spilling her drink; pretending to be a stool so that an old lady about to sit down to tell a sad story falls on the floor.

3 When you have discussed the three tricks, split the class into six groups. Ask three of the groups to create a **mime** showing one of the tricks. Encourage them to make the mimes as funny as possible.

4 Give the other three groups one each of the sections from pcm 26. Ask them to find a way of speaking the words as a group to make them sound interesting. Suggest that they could say some lines together and some individually and they could use different voices. Give them as much help as possible with the pronunciation but encourage them to spend more time on playing around with the words.

5 After some rehearsal, look at the mimes and listen to the readings group by group. Match the mimes to the appropriate reading and perform them for the rest of the class.

27 Romeo and Juliet

Drama space
Classroom or hall

 Subject link
History

Organisation
7 groups, groups of 3 or 4

Age
9–11

Note
You will need one whole copy of the pcm and one copy cut into the individual sections.

 pcm 27 on page 68

Purpose
● To encourage children to think about the relevance of Shakespeare's plays today.

Activities
1 Read the story of Romeo and Juliet to the children from pcm 27. Discuss their reactions to the story. You may wish to copy the breakdown of the characters onto a blackboard or flip chart.

2 Split the class into seven groups and give each group one of the headings on the pcm. Ask each group to create a **still image** to illustrate their section.

3 Put all the still images together to depict the story.

4 Discuss Romeo and Juliet's dilemma. Ask: *Can you think of one group of people who hate another group of people in today's world?*

Do any countries come to mind? Could the story of Romeo and Juliet happen today? If so, where and why might it happen? Do teenagers still do things secretly against their parents' wishes? If so, what sort of things? What might the consequences be?

5 After the discussion, split the class into groups of three or four. Ask each group to think about one of the following situations: Two teenagers want to date but their families are against it because they dislike each other. Two teenagers run away from home and things turn out badly.

6 Each groups creates a short **scene** depicting the situation and enacts it for the class.

7 Discuss the similarities and differences between these scenes and Shakespeare's Romeo and Juliet.

28 Memories

Drama space
Classroom or hall

Organisation
Individuals, pairs, small groups, whole class

Age
9–11

Purpose

● To gain awareness of the importance of memory.

Activities

1 Each child sits quietly on their own and thinks about something special that they remember from when they were younger. Encourage them to recall it in as much detail as they can.

2 In pairs, the children share their memories.

3 Working in small groups, each group creates a **still picture** of an important early memory, such as first steps, falling, spilling a drink, starting school. **Bring** them **to life** for a few seconds. Encourage the children to make the memories as real as possible.

4 Put all the still images together to create a whole-class drama by bringing the still pictures to life as you pass each group.

Further activities

▶ You can develop the memory theme in a number of ways, for example:

– Focus on old age and how important memory is to the elderly. The children could interview their grandparents or other elderly people they know.

– Use **ritual** and chants to expand the drama. You could also add dance.

 # 29 Pantomime

Drama space
Hall

Resources
Paper and pens or pencils

Organisation
Small groups

Age
9–11

Purpose

● To explore pantomime as a theatrical style.

Activities

1 Discuss pantomimes. *What do the children understand by the term? How many stories that are used for pantomime do they know?* Discuss one or two examples which children have seen either on television or in the theatre. Emphasise the elements that distinguish pantomime: a lively story, lots of slapstick comedy, exaggerated **characters**, women playing men, men playing women, lots of songs and audience involvement. Agree a pantomime for the class to work on.

(You might mention Aladdin, Mother Goose, Dick Whittington.)

2 In small groups, the children act one of the **scenes** from the selected play.

3 Share the scenes with the whole class and use the discussion in step 1 as a checklist. Is the scene really like a pantomime? How could it be made more so?

Further activities

▶ The children rework their scenes taking account of the views of the rest of the class as expressed in step 3. The groups perform the reworked scenes again.

30 **From book to stage**

Drama space
Classroom

Organisation
Individuals

Resources
pcm 19 on page 63;
pcm 24 on page 66;
pcm 54 on page 79

Age
11

Note
This is a very demanding activity and may require several sessions.

pcm 30 on page 69

Purpose
● To offer experience of creating a play script from prose.

Activities
1 Go through the procedure on pcm 30 together. Enlarge on the instructions there as follows:

– **1** means everything Lee and Mum say, either in thoughts or out loud.

– **2** means any descriptions of the setting, for example, there is a table in the kitchen and Lee must be sitting there.

– **3** means anything about the actions, for example, Lee must be looking at the envelope first; his mother has to walk into the kitchen a bit later.

– **4** Look at the pcms under Resources together and explain how to set the scene as these do. Refer also to your script (right) without showing it.

– **5** Refer to Resources and the script (right).

2 Check the child's first draft, suggesting improvements.

3 If a good script results, encourage a performance for the rest of the class.

Suggested script

A kitchen. Lee sits at the table. He is looking at a brown envelope and talking to himself.

Lee: The worst report – ever! What's Mum gonna say?

Mum: (Calling out of the room) Lee, I'm home.

Lee: Oh, no! This is it!

Lee looks at the letter. His mum is nearly at the kitchen. Lee quickly sits down, putting the letter on his chair and sitting on it.

Mum: Hello, love. Had a good day?

Lee: Oh, hello, Mum.

Mum: Make me a cup of tea will you, Lee? I'm tired out.

Lee half rises. Then sits down again. He can't think what to do.

Mum: Come on, love. I'm really tired. Please make the tea while I put this shopping away.

Lee: Well, you see, Mum.

The phone rings in another room. Mum leaves to answer it. Lee stands up quickly. He picks up the letter and shoves it in his pocket. As he does so, Mum returns.

Mum: That was your teacher, Lee. She asked if I had a chance to look at your report yet. She thinks I'll be concerned. Where is it?

All freeze

31 The sad clown

Drama space
Classroom

Subject link
English

Organisation
Whole class, pairs

Resources
Any picture of a clown; a clown's hat if available; copy of the note opposite prepared in advance

Age
5–7

Purpose

● To provide opportunities for exploring emotions and solving problems by working together.

Activities

1 As a class, look at the picture and choose a name for the clown. Discuss why the clown looks sad. List the possible reasons.

2 **In role** as the sad clown, put on a clown's hat if you have one. Invite the class to question you about why you are sad. Try not to say anything specific, but simply respond with a despondent nod or shake of the head, so that your reason for sadness remains a mystery.

3 In pairs, the children work on ways to make you laugh or smile using **mime** actions. As you work in a circus, the pairs could mime funny circus acts. When they show their mimes, you may laugh or smile momentarily but maintain the mood of sadness.

4 Still in role, produce the note from your pocket and read it out. Everyone tries to think of ways to save the circus. Still in role, discuss this together, agree on a plan and act it out. This idea could be returned to over several days and could include drama, dance, music, artwork and writing. One possibility is to develop a procession with the participants handing out publicity while singing and dancing.

> Dear Clowns,
>
> I am sorry to tell you that the circus must close. Not enough people are coming to see our shows any more. So this is your last week as a clown.
>
> The owner

32 In the playground

Drama space
Classroom or hall

Organisation
Small groups, whole class

Age
5–9

Purpose

● To focus on what happens at playtime and how the class can help to make it fun for everyone.

Activities

1 Each child thinks of something that they do at playtime and **mimes** this within a whole-class **scene.**

2 In groups of three or four, the children think of all the different sounds and words they hear at playtime. They use these to create a **sound collage**. You might conduct the groups individually or all together to create different levels of sound.

3 In their groups, the children think of things that cause trouble in the playground and create a **still picture** of the moment the trouble starts. You then move from group to group asking individuals what they are thinking or saying.

4 As a whole class, discuss the problems and fears related to playtime. How can the class and the school work together to overcome these?

33 Ruler of the world

Drama space
Classroom

Subject link
English

Organisation
Whole class

Resources
A small bag

Age
5–7

Purpose

● To investigate the responsible exercise of power.

Activities

1 Explain that you have some magic dust in your bag. If you rub some between your fingers, you become Ruler of the World and everyone has to do what you say. Explain that they will act out what you command. If, for example, you say everyone must brush their teeth, then everyone must **mime** brushing their teeth. Explain that you will rub the magic dust between your fingers on each new command. Run through a few commands, using ideas that are clear and easily acted, such as:

'The Ruler of the World says you must jump up and down five times.'

'The Ruler of the World says you must be still and silent.'

'The Ruler of the World says you must sing a song.'

2 Allow a few children turns at being Ruler of the World. Encourage them to think of clear, easily followed commands.

3 Look into the bag and say that there is only enough magic dust for two more rubs. Ask the children to think of a command, and challenge each idea. Try to develop the notion that it might not be fair to give one person the power to rule everyone. See if it is possible to agree on a command. Think through all the implications of the command and discuss its consequences.

4 Now there is one magic rub left. You can use this to undo the last command, if the class think that is best, by saying, *'The Ruler of the World says you do not have to obey the last command'*. Or you can save it for another time.

34 Signs

Drama space
Classroom

Subject link
English

Organisation
Pairs, whole class

Age
5–7

Purpose

● To encourage the children to explore alternative means of communication.

Activities

1 In pairs, ask the children to find a way of saying hello to each other without speaking. Share these ideas.

2 Discuss when signing might be used, for example, when there is loud noise, among the deaf, controlling traffic, waving to a friend.

3 Read one of the simple messages (right). Ask the children, in pairs, to work out a way of communicating this message to each other without words. Encourage them to provide as much detail as possible. Try as many of the messages as there is time for.

4 Sitting in a circle, ask each child to sign a simple message which the rest of the class has to work out. With young children, you could suggest the beginning of the message, for example, *'I like …'* or *'I am good at …'*

Further activities

▶ Look at and practise British sign language.

Suggested messages

– Meet me at two o'clock.

– I am hungry.

– I am too hot.

– What is the time?

– I am angry with you.

– Would you like an apple?

35 Welcome to our school

Drama space
Classroom

Organisation
Whole class, pairs, groups

Age
5–7

Purposes
● To practice reassuring a nervous person.
● To think about how to make the school more welcoming to newcomers.

Activities
1 Discuss what makes your school a happy place. Draw out a few specifics such as bright artwork, kind teachers, friendly children, a good playground.

2 In pairs, the children create a short **scene** showing one child being friendly and helpful to another.
3 Ask the children to imagine that a new child is to join their class. In groups, they think of one idea for helping him/her to feel welcome and at home.
4 Discuss the ideas and, if appropriate, **role play** some of them.

36 Who is safe?

Drama space
Classroom

Organisation
Whole class, small groups

Age
5–9

Note
This is a sensitive area in which school policies differ. These suggestions are offered to indicate how drama might be integrated into your school policy.

Purpose
● To suggest how drama can be used to support the school's Safety with Strangers policy.

Activities
1 Discuss the kind of situation in which children might find it difficult to know what to do, particularly in relation to requests from adults. Elicit children's suggestions. Ask small groups to act out the suggestions either as a **mime**, a **still picture** or a short **scene**.
2 Practice situations in which children need to say no to adults, for example:

– A stranger offers a lift.
– A stranger offers sweets.
– A stranger asks a child to go to an known danger area (canal, steep drop or something appropriate to your school location).
In pairs, children enact the situations, swapping roles so that each gets the chance to say no.
3 In a circle, discuss difficult situations the children can think of. Encourage them always to talk with responsible adults about anything that worries them.

37 Summer holiday

Drama space
Hall or classroom

 Subject link
English

Organisation
Small groups

Age
5–7

Purpose
● To build a simple drama around the theme of holidays.

Activities
1 Talk about holidays. Explain that you are going to do some drama about going on holiday to the seaside.
2 In small groups, children decide what they would need to take for a week.
3 In their groups, children create **still pictures**, for example, making sand

castles on the beach, paddling in the sea, riding donkeys.
4 Say that it has started to rain. What can they do? Still in their groups, the children create still pictures, showing what they did when the rain began.
5 Finally, the children create a simple **mime** on their favourite part of the holiday. Each group shows their mime to the class.

38 I want to be...

Drama space
Classroom

Organisation
Whole class, pairs

Age
7–11

Purpose
● To introduce the world of work and help children to focus on ambitions and careers.

Activities
1 Discuss work and jobs. Elicit the children's ideas about jobs they would like to do.
2 In pairs, one child plays a person who has just won an award for excellence in their job. The other child plays a newspaper, radio or TV reporter interviewing him or her to find out why they are so keen on their job and how they became so good at it.

Further activities
► Talk about qualifications for various careers.

39 I know what you're thinking

Drama space
Classroom or hall

Organisation
Whole class, small groups

Age
7–11

pcm 39 on page 70

Purposes
● To explore how what people say can differ from what they're thinking.
● To focus on times when it is best to keep thoughts private.

Activities
1 Talk about the idea of people saying one thing while thinking another. Examples might include: singing a song in assembly while thinking about playtime.
2 In small groups, the children work from pcm 39 to create a short **scene** in which they **freeze** the actions at some point. During the freezes, one or more of the characters speak their secret thoughts before the scene **comes to life** again. The groups decide who will speak.
3 Use the best of the scenes as the basis for a discussion about politeness and when it might be better to keep thoughts private.

40 Bullying

Drama space
Classroom or hall

Organisation
Whole class, small groups

Age
7–11

Purpose
● To open up the issue of bullying and suggest strategies for dealing with it.

Activities
1 Begin with a class discussion of what is meant by bullying. In small groups, ask the children to decide what can start this sort of trouble at school.
2 In the same groups, ask them to create a still picture of someone being bullied while others either participate or watch. They must each know who they are and what they are doing.
3 Each groups shows their **still picture** to the whole class without introduction. You ask the class if they can understand what is being shown. Then the class can ask the **characters** what they are thinking or what they are saying.
4 Chose one group's idea to work with for the rest of the session. The class should decide whether to back track to where the situation started or move towards some sort of resolution. They need to ask questions of, and direct the characters, in the still image. They may also need to bring in new characters as appropriate. Are there a number of different solutions?

Further activities
► Ask the class how they think an adult could have helped in the dramatised situation. Ask one group to create a still picture of the best moment for an adult to intervene. Do the others agree with the group? What else might be done? Which adults would be most helpful?

41 Under the microscope

Drama space
Hall

Subject link
English

Organisation
Individuals, small groups, whole class

Age
7–9

Purpose
- To encourage the social health of the class by focusing on the class as a whole in a light-hearted way.

Activities

1 Ask each child to describe the class. Suggest such ideas as: Sometimes our class is noisy. Our class is the best. We're excellent at sport. Sometimes we argue too much. We look after each other.

2 Develop these into an agreed list.

3 In small groups, ask the children to prepare an exaggerated action and/or sound expressing one of the ideas. For example:

– Sometimes our class is noisy. They could shout the word 'noisy' and whisper the rest.

– Our class is the best. The group could walk around with an exaggerated swagger.

– We're excellent at sport. They could mime receiving a medal.

4 Use all the dramatised ideas to create a performance called 'Our class under the microscope'.

42 Runaway

Drama space
Classroom or hall

Organisation
Three groups, then pairs

Resources
A bag containing Joe's note, the get well card and a purse containing £1

Age
7–11

pcm 42 on page 71

Purpose
- To raise awareness of the causes and consequences of running away.

Activities

1 In role as a police officer or a social worker, talk about Joe, a young boy who has run away from home. Say that he had dropped his bag in the process, and it was handed in to you.

2 Say that one of the things in the bag was the letter on pcm 42. Come out of role.

3 Discuss what the letter might have had to do with Joe's disappearance.

Ask: *Do you think Joe's parents ever got the letter? Do you think Joe was afraid of his parents? Would such a letter be enough to make someone run away?*

4 Divide the class into small groups. Each enact a short **scene** showing what might have happened to make Joe run away.

Further activities
► In pairs, the children stage a telephone conversation between a Child Line counsellor and Joe, who has called to discuss his problems.

43 Rules

Drama space
Classroom or hall

Organisation
Whole class, small groups

Resources
The school rules

Age
7–11

Purpose
- To examine the nature and value of rules at school.

Activities

1 Look at the school rules and discuss them with the class. The nature of the discussion will depend on the type of rules your school has, but in general, guide the discussion to a consideration of whether the rules are sensible and clear.

2 In small groups, ask the children to choose one of the rules and enact a short **scene** showing that rule being broken.

3 The class look at the scenes performed in turn and discuss them. In each case, the class decides what the consequences should be for those who break the rule.

Further activities
► Discuss how the school would function if there were no rules. *Would it function well? Would people know what was right and wrong?* In their groups, the children enact a scene in which one of them does something that the others believe is wrong, but there are no rules about it. What can they do?

► Once more, the groups perform their scenes in turn and they are discussed. Would it have been better if there were rules?

44 Self esteem

Drama space
Classroom

Organisation
Whole class

Age
7–9

Purposes
● To encourage self-esteem.
● To help children express themselves openly.

Activities
1 In a circle, explain that there are some ground rules for the activity that follows. These are:
– No one should laugh at or make fun of anything that is said or bring it up later, particularly in the playground.
– No one must say anything negative about themselves or anyone else.
– No one should disagree with anyone else's comments.
You may develop other rules as appropriate to your class if you think it necessary.
2 First, ask everyone to think of something they are good at. Then, as you go round the circle, each child says, 'I am good at …' Discuss whether or not the children found this easy or difficult, and why.
3 Next, ask everyone to think of something they like about themselves. This might be appearance or personality, for example, *'What I like about myself is that I'm small'*, or *'What I like about myself is my sense of humour'*.
4 Finally, go round the circle one by one, each time asking the others to say something they like about the child in question. This will take some time and might be something to return to on several occasions. If someone can't find anything positive to say, this should be gently and sensitively discussed rather than overlooked.

45 Telling the truth

Drama space
Classroom or hall

Organisation
Whole class, individuals

Age
7–9

pcm 45 on page 72

Purposes
● To consider the value of honesty.
● To provide positive strategies to help children value telling the truth.

Activities
1 Hand out pcm 45. Point out that Laura is a fictional character but the details are realistic. Discuss Laura's dilemma: her mum's guidance to tell the truth always, against her brother's advice to lie and her fear of the consequences if she doesn't.
2 Set up a **conscience alley** to decide what Laura should do when her mother comes home. One of the children takes the role of Laura. If the pro-truth line falters, you might suggest: *'Your mum'll find out'; 'Get it over with'; 'You know you should be honest'*. If the pro-lie line falters, you might suggest: *'No one will know'; 'Your mum'll believe you'; 'It's only a little lie'*. At the end of the line, Laura should make her decision based on the advice given.
3 Now act out the **scene** when Laura's mother comes home by means of **forum theatre**. You may wish to play Mum and the Laura character must abide by the decision she reached after the conscience alley. Perhaps her mother will make it difficult for her, either by not listening or getting angry. You can try the scene several times with different children taking the roles. You may want to introduce Ben and/or Laura's father into the scene.

46 Football for girls

Drama space
Classroom

Organisation
Individuals or pairs, small groups

Resources
Tape recorder or video camera
if available

Age
9–11

pcm 46 on page 73

Purposes
● To challenge gender stereotypes.
● To stimulate a range of written work.

Activities

1 Hand out pcm 46 and read Liam's monologue to the class. Ask for a volunteer to take the role of Liam or take it yourself and put Liam in the **hot seat**. Discourage trick questions or ones Liam couldn't be expected to answer

2 In pairs or small groups, the children write a monologue for Charlotte giving her point of view.

3 List all the possible characters in the story. These might include Charlotte, members of her football team, members of Liam's team, Charlotte and Liam's families. In pairs, one plays a reporter for a newspaper or TV interviewing one or more of these **characters**. The interviews could be taped on audio or video.

4 Ask the children to work alone or in pairs to write an account of Charlotte's first game for the girl's football team. Encourage them to make this as lively as possible. They should think about the atmosphere inside the ground. They might include snippets from the interview in addition to a description of the game.

5 In small groups, the children as newspaper reporters write an article on the team at the end of the season. They also think of a headline. Emphasise that the report should be balanced and contain opinions from different viewpoints. They can decide what might have been the progress of the team since Charlotte's first game. They can also create a **still picture** to be the photo accompanying the article.

47 Friendship

Drama space
Classroom or hall

Organisation
Pairs, whole class

Age
9–11

pcm 47 on page 74

Purpose
● To explore how to disagree with others without falling out or saying hurtful things.

Activities

1 Hand out pcm 47 and allow time for a short discussion in twos. Ask each pair to answer: *What is the letter about? What might have developed to make M write the letter?*

2 Develop step 1 into a class discussion.
3 The same pairs develop a short clear **scene** depicting one key incident that led up to the letter. You may need to give guidance about what is acceptable: no fighting or pushing, for example. Visit the pairs as they work and choose three or four of the best scenes to show the rest of the class. Discuss how each scene might have ended with a more positive outcome.
4 Ask the pairs to rework their scenes if the outcome had been negative. The pairs can be enlarged to small groups. The new scenes can be shown to the rest of the class.

Dear David,
I don't want to be your friend any more so please stop hanging around me at breaktime. With this letter are the two books you lent me. Please don't ask me why, you know why.
M.

48 The image box

Drama space
Classroom or hall

Organisation
Whole class, small groups

Resources
A box containing a number of items which have strong associations with image, for example, a pair of sunglasses, a baseball hat, a personal stereo, a teen magazine, a can of drink, a scruffy jumper, a torn plastic bag, a bar of chocolate, a lipstick

Age
9–11

Purposes
● To raise awareness of the concept of image and identity.

Activities
1 Talk about what is meant by image. *Which famous people have a good or positive image? Which famous people have a bad or negative image?*
2 Talk about the different items in the box. What sort of image is associated with each?
3 Ask for a volunteer to stand by. The rest of the class chooses three items from the Image Box that create a character with a negative image. Then the volunteer character wears or holds them. Discuss why these items were selected.
4 Do the same thing with a new character and a positive image, again discussing the reasons for the items.
5 In small groups, the children create short **scenes,** such as a job interview, a family wedding, a school outing, prize giving. They enact the scenes twice, once with the positive character and once with the negative. Discuss reactions to the characters' appearance and behaviour. Ask: *Are appearances really a good guide to a person's nature?*

 # 49 Nobody likes me!

Drama space
Classroom or hall

Organisation
Pairs, whole class, groups of 3 or 4

Age
9–11

pcm 49 on page 75

Purposes
● To explore feelings of isolation and loneliness.
● To suggest positive ways of dealing with these emotions.

Activities
1 Read pcm 49 to the whole class. Ask a child to read Sam, or ask two good readers to read both parts.
2 In pairs, the children work out some advice to give Sam. Then one takes the **role** of the counsellor and the other of Sam. Read the pcm again and ask different pairs to pick up from the point at which the script ends.
3 Discuss the different advice that Sam was given.
4 In groups of three or four, the groups dramatise ways in which Sam could begin to resolve her problem. One pupil could be Sam, another Rebecca and the others their classmates. Try to ensure that the **scenes** end positively.
5 Each group enacts their scene for the class.

50 Smoking

Drama space
Classroom or hall

Organisation
Small groups

Age
9–11

pcm 50 on page 76

Purposes
● To open the issue of young people smoking.
● To provide positive strategies to stop children smoking.

Activities
1 Hand out copies of pcm 50. Point out that Toni is a fictional character but the details are realistic. Read the monologue and discuss the issues it raises.
2 In small groups, the children create **still pictures** based on such situations as:
– the moment Toni has her first cigarette
– a surgeon carrying out a lung cancer operation
– a young person saying no to smoking.
3 Discuss any insights the still images have given.

4 Focus upon Toni's words:
'I mean one fag... it's not as if I'm addicted, is it?' Set up a **conscience alley** to help Toni decide if she will smoke again. One line should give reasons why she should not smoke again. (*'It could kill you'. 'It's a waste of money'. 'It makes your breath smell'.*) The other line uses peer pressure to encourage her to carry on smoking. (*'It's only a laugh'. 'Everyone does it'. 'If you want to do it, do it'.*) Toni reaches her decision.
5 Ask the children what they think would help them decide not to smoke.
6 In groups, the children produce TV and radio advertisements, posters or presentations to persuade young people not to smoke.

51 Our island

Drama space
Hall

Subject link
Geography

Organisation
Groups of 5 or 6

Resources
Coloured felt-tip pens

Age
9–11

Note
If possible, enlarge the pcm to A3 size.

pcm 51 on page 77

Purposes
● To develop skills in decision making, negotiation and co-operation.
● To encourage thinking about environmental issues.

Activities
1 In groups of five or six (preferably a mix of boys and girls), the children imagine that they have been shipwrecked on an island. Ask them to create two **still images**, the first showing the shipwreck and the second showing their initial reaction to the island.
2 Give each group a copy of pcm 51 along with some coloured felt-tip pens and ask each group to work out where and how they would build shelters. *Would they build one or several? Should they be near water, food, or something else?*

3 Ask them to make a list of the day-to-day jobs that would need doing and to allocate these jobs. Discuss each group's choices and the reasons behind them.
4 Ask each group to decide on a list of rules that would make life on the island safe and happy. Encourage them to think about how they would enforce these rules in a fair way.
5 Ask them to imagine that someone has broken one of the rules. Each group should set up a court with a judge, prosecutor, defender, witnesses and the accused. Encourage each person to rehearse what they will say. Enact the court **scenes**. The rest of the class acts as a jury and brings in their verdict. Then the judge decides what action should be taken, bearing in mind that everyone on the island is needed to contribute to the workload.

52 Drug dilemmas

Drama space
Classroom or hall

Subject link
Science

Organisation
Whole class, groups of 4

Resources
The different choices listed written on separate pieces of paper in advance

Age
9–11

pcm 52 on page 78

Purposes
● To raise and examine drug related issues.
● To empower children to make informed choices.

Activities
1 Read the story on pcm 52 with the class, then discuss the choices listed.

Choices
– Jo accuses the others of being stupid and goes home.

– Jo tries to persuade the others to stop because they'll get into trouble.

– Jo tries to persuade the others to stop because of the dangers of drinking.

– Jo takes a large swig and feels sick.

– Jo has a drink and pretends to enjoy it.

– Jo has a drink and hates the taste.

– Jo says no and tells the others that it's up to each person to decide for themselves.

– Jo doesn't have a drink but tries to make a joke of the situation.

– Jo goes to tell an adult that the others are drinking.

2 In groups of four, the children enact the **scene** up to the point where Alex offers Jo a drink.
3 Give the child playing Jo in each group one of the slips of paper containing a different choice. The rest of the group should not see it.
4 Ask each group to enact the scene for the rest of the class. Jo reacts according to the choice given. Ensure that the rest of the group understands that their behaviour should be appropriate to Jo's decision. Continue each scene until some sort of conclusion is reached.
5 Discuss which choice the children felt led to the best conclusion and why.

53 Ad for a dad

Drama space
Classroom or hall

Organisation
Whole class, pairs, then pairs or small groups

Age
9–11

Purpose

● To explore the child-parent relationship.

Activities

1 Read Simon's monologue (see right) aloud and elicit the children's reaction to it: Does it seem strange that Simon says he was not upset when his father died? Do you believe him? Do you think his idea was good? Why is the newspaper interested? Will it upset his mother? Why hasn't he told his mother what he did?

2 In pairs, the children act out the **scene** in which Simon tells his mother about the advertisement and the interview. Each pair shows their scene to the rest of the class. Discuss what the scenes have revealed about Simon and his mother.

3 In pairs or small groups, the children write the newspaper report and an attention-grabbing headline.

4 In the same pairs or groups, they devise the photograph accompanying the article as a **still picture**.

5 Discuss whether it is a good idea to advertise as Simon did. What does the future hold for Simon?

> **Simon is 11 years old and is thinking about what he has just done.**
>
> 'My dad died six months ago. I wasn't too upset. I know I shouldn't say that but it's true. We never got on. He worked nights and weekends and when he was around he just seemed to shout at me all the time. My mum was upset, though. Only now she seems to be getting over it.
>
> A few weeks ago I began thinking what it would be like to have a new dad. Somebody who would take me to football matches and go fishing with me.
>
> I was looking in this newspaper at the pages with adverts. Free adverts. You could just send one in. I had this idea. Why not put in an ad for a new dad? So I did. I sent in an advert saying I wanted a new dad. Next day the phone rings. My mum was out so I answered it. It was the newspaper about my advert. They wanted to come round to our house. Wanted to ask me some questions and take a photo. I said yes. So they're coming tomorrow. Trouble is, I haven't told Mum about it and I don't know what to do next.'

54 Odd one out

Drama space
Classroom or hall

Organisation
Whole class, pairs

Age
9–11

pcm 54 on page 79

Purpose

● To examine the tensions within the family.

Activities

1 Read pcm 54. Reread it a couple of times with different children taking the roles. You could also set up a table and chairs and act out the **scene**.

2 Discuss the issues. *Is Peter being fair? Is his mum being fair?*

3 In pairs, one child plays Peter and one Mum. (Or it could be a girl in the same situation and her mum or dad.) They are to pick up the story immediately after the scene they have just read. First they decide where each **character** is. Perhaps Peter is sulking in his bedroom or outside the door or running down the street. Mum could still be at the table or

outside looking for Peter or starting to eat. Explain that one character is to speak their thoughts briefly, then **freeze** while the other character speaks their thoughts. Encourage them to work out a dramatic scene in this way, with each character speaking their thoughts a couple of times.

4 After some pairs show their scenes (as many as there is time for), discuss what might happen when Peter and his mum are together again. *What will they say to each other? Can the class think of ways that will help them to deal with the problem?*

Further activities

► The ideas in step 4 could be written as further scenes or enacted by **improvisation**.

55 Fear

Drama space
Classroom or hall

Organisation
Pairs, whole class

Age
9–11

Purpose
● To explore feelings of fear.

Activities
1 In pairs, the children first talk about and then create a situation in which one person feels fear or a strong sense of insecurity, such as worrying about school work; being bullied; seeing a gang waiting for them. The pairs create short dramatic **scenes** of their situation. Suggest that it might be a good idea to start and end the scenes with a **still picture** to help structure them. Stress the importance of clearly depicting the exact moment of fear.

2 After each pair shows their scene, discuss them, also giving ideas for helping.

Further activity
▶ If appropriate, further drama can be developed from the discussion with the emphasis on how to avoid or defuse threatening situations.

56 Head shaved

Drama space
Classroom or hall

Organisation
Whole class, pairs

Age
9–11

pcm 56 on page 80

Purposes
● To explore the notions of personal appearance in schools.

Activities
1 Read pcm 56 together and discuss the children's response to it. What sort of person does Karlo seem to be? Would they have him as a friend? Did the school act sensibly?

2 Working in pairs, the children devise one of two scenes:

– The headteacher sends Karlo home from school.

– Karlo tells his mum or dad what has happened.

3 Set up a **conscience alley**. Individuals in one line try to persuade Karlo to shave off his logo; the other line tries to persuade him to keep it. Karlo makes his decision.

4 In a circle, Karlo **in role** is in the middle. Karlo explains his decision to the rest of the class. They respond to his decision collectively as his mates.

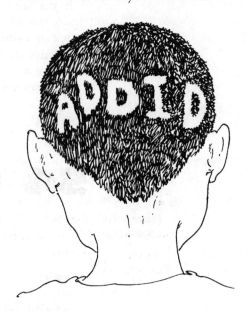

57 New school

Drama space
Hall or classroom

Organisation
Whole class, pairs, 3 groups

Age
11+

Purposes

● To explore children's concerns about changing schools.

● To support them at a potentially difficult time.

Activities

1 The class sit in a circle, the centre of which is the drama space. Explain that they are going to create a giant sculpture called New School. One by one the children add themselves to the sculpture and **freeze** in a pose showing how they feel on the first day at a new school. Altogether they form a **still picture**.

2 Ask a few children at a time to come out of the sculpture and study it before returning to their places.

3 Sit in the circle again and talk about the sculpture. Are there some poses that reflect real fears?

4 Talk about fears and concerns that children may have about going to a new school.

5 In pairs, the children hold a phone conversation on the night before they both are going to a new school. One of them is worried about a particular thing (not knowing the teacher; wondering where the toilets are; hoping to be liked) and the friend should try to reassure them.

6 Split the class into three groups. Group 1: older children coming back to school; they are relaxed and chatty. Group 2: new pupils who are with friends; they are pleasurably excited. Group 3: new pupils on their own; they are nervous and feel lonely. Ask the groups to mix together in the drama space, which is to represent the playground. They are to form a still image called First Day of Term.

7 Swap groups and re-form the still image. Walk in the midst of the still picture and ask individuals to speak their thoughts.

8 Unfreeze the picture and discuss how each group could help those who are nervous and lonely, and what individuals could do to help themselves.

9 Re-form the still image and try some of the ideas suggested in step 8 by **bringing the picture to life**.

 # 58 Old schooldays

Drama space
Classroom

Organisation
Whole class, small groups

Age
5–9

Purpose

● To use drama in a history context by finding out about the schooldays of the children's parents.

Activities

1 Ask the children to talk to their parents about their schooldays, or invite some parents into school to talk about their school experiences. Encourage the children to ask questions about the games their elders played, what they studied, what are the biggest differences between then and now.

2 Learn and play some of the old games mentioned. These could be put together to create a playground **scene**.

3 Focus on clear differences between then and now: the use of computers might be a good example. In small groups, each group creates two sets of **still pictures**, one showing THEN and the other NOW. Put these together to create whole-class still pictures, which change as you call 'then' and 'now'.

59 Pharaoh's footsteps

Drama space
Classroom or hall

Subject link
RE

Organisation
Whole class, then individuals or small groups

Resources
Large piece of paper; paint

Background
Some knowledge of ancient Egypt

Age
7–11

Note
Step 1 may need a session on its own.

pcm 59 on page 81

Purpose
● To examine the morality of disturbing an ancient site.

Activities

1 Take on the role of the supervisor responsible for preparing Tutankhamun's tomb. Pass out the pieces of paper. Ask the children, as tomb workers, to create paintings to go on the floor of the tomb, using pcm 59 as a reference for the designs.

2 Arrange the completed pictures on the floor. Ask the children to create **still pictures** of everyday Egyptian life to go on the walls of the tomb.

3 As the chief tomb worker, declare that *Death shall come on swift wing to whosoever shall disturb this tomb.*

4 **Out of role**, explain that you are going to move the drama thousands of years to 1922 when Howard Carter unearthed the tomb of Tutankhamun.

5 Ask the children to create a whole-class still image of Howard Carter, Lord Carnarvon and journalists watching as the tomb is being opened.

6 Talk about whether it was right for Howard Carter to disturb a pharaoh's grave. Was he a great archaeologist or a tomb robber?

7 Put Howard Carter in the **hot seat**. The role of Howard Carter can be taken by you, an individual child or a small group of children. Guide the questioning so that the issue of right and wrong is brought out.

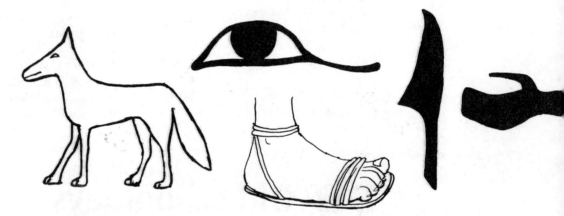

60 Roman remains

Drama space
Hall

Resources
A fragment of pottery, as old looking as possible

Organisation
Whole class, individuals

Age
7–11

Purpose
● To begin to understand the Roman times in Britain.

Activities

1 In a circle, address the children as if they were archaeologists. You say that an old piece of pottery has been found in a nearby field. It may be of Roman origin but no one is sure. The piece of pottery is passed from hand to hand round the circle for comments. Elicit comments about the age of the fragment, its texture, colour, possible size of the whole piece, possible form of the whole piece.

2 The children, **in role**, move to a space which represents the field where the piece of pottery was found. They are to **mime** a search of the area, being extremely careful to look for objects which are interesting. Three small areas

at the edge of the room are indicated for placing their finds. These are to be designated for:
– objects thought to be Roman
– modern objects clearly not Roman
– objects needing further consideration.

3 Still in role, each child in turn describes what they have found. Any object of uncertain date is further discussed. **Out of role**, the children think about what might have happened in this area back in Roman times.

4 In role, the children take the drama back in time and create individual **still pictures** showing how the found objects might have been used. You can **bring** the still pictures **to life** for a few seconds if this is appropriate. Or, after each still image, the rest of the children could make up a **caption**.

61 Victorian servants

Drama space
Hall

 Subject links
PSHE, English

Organisation
Whole class, pairs

Resources
Optional: samples of Victorian servants' clothing; archive material

Age
7–11

Purpose

● To gain some understanding of a servant's life in Victorian times.

Activities

1 Ask the children what they know about being a servant in Victorian times. You might pose specific questions such as: *Who had servants? Where did the servants come from? Where did the servants live? What were their living conditions like? What kinds of jobs might a servant do? Were they paid well?*

2 In a large space, the children practice curtseying or bowing until they reach a standard you set. Come together and recap the type of jobs a servant would do. Each child chooses a job to do and **mimes** doing it. You may need to make suggestions to assure a wide spread of jobs. After a few minutes, stop the action and choose two children to be a wealthy couple. They walk about the space as the servants work. Begin the action again. The servants must stand respectfully when one of the couple comes near and

bow or curtsey as they pass. Swap roles from time to time.

3 In pairs, one child is the rich person, the other is the servant. They enact this **scene**: The rich person sits on a chair, summons the servant, and gives the servant a task from those discussed in steps 1 and 2. After a while the rich person examines the results of the servant's work and passes appropriate comment. (Remind the servant always to obey and accept criticism meekly. Remind the employer not to be cruel or provocative, even if unreasonable.) You may decide to demonstrate with one child first. Switch roles within the pairs and repeat the scene.

4 Together, **out of role**, discuss the experience of being a servant, focusing on the feelings induced by the **role play**.

Further activities

▶ Follow this with a writing activity in which a new servant writes home after his or her first day at the Big House.

62 Victorian children

Drama space
Hall or classroom

Organisation
Groups of 5 or 6

Age
7–9

Note:
You will need only enough copies of the pcm for yourself and each group.

pcm 62 on page 82

Purpose

● To compare some aspects of the lives of children today with children of the same age in the Victorian era.

Activities

1 Read aloud together the four descriptions of children's lives in the Victorian era on pcm 62. Discuss some of the differences between being rich and poor in that period.

2 In groups of five or six, ask the children to choose one of the Victorian lives you have read to them. Hand out copies of the pcm. In their groups, the children prepare a **still picture** to illustrate one aspect of the lives described.

3 In the same groups, the children prepare a still picture based on a similar aspect of their own lives (for example, school, any housework they do, toys and games).

4 In the groups, ask the children to make one list of words which describes the Victorian still picture and one list

which describes the modern picture. Using these words, each group creates a short poem about the differences between the two still pictures and, therefore, between the two eras.

Further activities

▶ These poems could be recorded.

▶ A narrator could read the poem while the group re-forms the two still pictures as appropriate to the words.

63 Viking raids

Drama space
Classroom or hall

Organisation
Small groups; whole class

Resources
Two large pieces of paper;
coloured felt-tip pens

Background
Some knowledge of the Vikings

Age
7–11

Note
The drama is intended to extend
and consolidate previous learning.

Purpose
● To focus on Viking raids in Britain and to consider the resistance offered by the Anglo-Saxons.

Activities
1 Take two very large sheets of paper and draw a rough outline of a Viking ship or warrior on each. In two groups, ask the children to fill the inside of the outline with words that express characteristics of Vikings, such as 'fierce', 'adventurous', 'good sailors', and pictures, such as shields, helmets, furry clothes. Discuss the words and pictures.
2 **In role** as an Anglo-Saxon chief of a village, say you have heard the Vikings are coming on a raid. Organise a village **meeting** to discuss whether to resist by fighting or whether to try to meet the Vikings to talk about a peaceful settlement. Try to make a decision as a whole group.
3 In small groups, or as a whole class, create a **still picture** to show the future of the village based on the decision in step 2. Possible pictures are: a destroyed and looted village with a handful of injured survivors; a victory celebration; a meeting of surrender; a life of slavery; a peaceful life.

64 Life on the canal

Drama space
Classroom

Organisation
Whole class, small groups

Age
7–9

Purpose
● To raise awareness about one aspect of life during the industrial revolution.

Activities
1 Talk about the kind of things a child would have to do on a barge during the 19th century and then **narrate** a **movement sequence**:
– Getting up before sun up. It is cold and the barge is frozen in.
– Breaking the ice with sticks.
– Harnessing the horse and leading it along the bank as it pulls the barge (still bitterly cold).
– Loading heavy bales of cloth.
– Setting off again, eating a crust of bread.
– Legging through a long tunnel. (Legging means lying on your back and pushing against the tunnel walls with your legs.)
2 Narrate three whole-class **still pictures** showing increasing tiredness as the day goes on.
3 In family groups, ask the children to discuss the following:
The local vicar wants one of the children to go to school. The family must decide whether to allow this.
In their family groups, the children enact a **scene** in which one of the parents comes into the barge directly after speaking with the vicar and states the problem. The family must decide quickly what to do, based on the for and against arguments below.

FOR	AGAINST
– The child is bright and will benefit from schooling.	– The child is needed to work on the barge.
– In time, an educated child could help the family by handling money, dealing with suppliers, and so on.	– The family will have to buy books and has little money.
– This is a chance that may never come again.	– The child would not be able to live at home because the barge is always on the move.

65 The blitz

Drama space
Classroom or hall

Organisation
Whole class, individuals, pairs

Resources
Tape recorder if desired

Age
9–11

pcm 65 on page 83

Purpose

● To explore the emotions of people who experienced the blitz.

Activities

1 Provide everyone with a copy of pcm 65. Explain that this is a fictional eye witness account of the blitz of a British town in May 1941. Read the account together and ask the children to say what impresses them the most.

2 Individually, the children try to imagine themselves as the eye witness. Ask them to focus upon the senses and as they imagine the sights, sounds and smells, form a few **still pictures**.

3 In pairs, one child is a radio or newspaper interviewer trying to find out what happened. (There was no TV at that time.) The other is someone who experienced the blitz. Individually again, they prepare for their role. The interviewer needs to think about what questions to ask. Remind this role player to be aware that the person they will meet might be in a state of shock and might not be able to answer all the questions. The eye witness should decide on a name and age, background, where they were when the bombing took place and if they are in shock. If in shock, their replies might be confused.

4 **Role play** the interviews. You may wish to tape record them and, if there is enough time, have the pairs swap roles. Come out of the drama.

5 The children organise a **meeting** for those who have lost their homes in the blitz to decide what can be done to help.

6 Read the account again. Although it is of a British town in 1941 it could be about almost any bombing. What are the common features?

Further activities

► Research further into the period to find out what actually happened during World War II bombings.

66 Charles I and the Civil War

Drama space
Classroom or hall

Organisation
Whole class, pairs, groups of 4

Resources
A large old key; a blindfold

Age
9–11

Purpose
● To help consolidate knowledge of the Civil War.

Activities
1 Begin with a game of Keeper of the Keys. In a circle, one child is keeper of the keys, blindfolded with the big old key on the floor close to them. The object of the game is for someone to take the key away from the blindfolded keeper and return to their place without making a sound. If the keeper hears a sound, she or he points in the direction of the sound. If correct, the thief has to return to their place empty handed and another thief is chosen. A successful thief becomes the next keeper. You choose consecutive thieves as necessary.

2 After a few turns, you take the key and ask the children to imagine that it belongs to one of the rooms in Carrisbrooke Castle on the Isle of Wight. Charles I is a prisoner there after losing the Civil War. Explain that the next part of the drama will focus upon a dream that Charles is having. It is filled with flashbacks to the horrors of the war. Ask each child to sit alone and close their eyes. Read the following text.

> Thou wouldest think it strange if I should tell thee there was a time in England when brothers killed brothers, cousins their cousins, and friends their friends. Nay, when they considered it no offence to commit murder. To murder a man, woman or child, held less offence than to kill a dog.

Then ask the children to create a **sound montage** of the war with sounds such as galloping horses, cries of the wounded, snatches of conversation, Charles's thoughts. Begin the montage with everyone's eyes closed, then discuss what has been created and, **in role** as conductor, practise the montage with everyone's eyes open.

3 In pairs, try to plan an escape.

4 Enlarge the pairs into groups of four and allow them to talk over the two previous plans. They choose one of them and work on a short **scene** showing how it was tried and failed.

Further activity
► Charles I was imprisoned in Carisbrooke for just over a year very near the end of his life. Find out what happened to him after he left the castle.

67 Emigration

Drama space
Classroom or hall

Subject links
Geography, Art

Organisation
Whole class, groups, individuals

Resources
Several postcards of
The Last of England, painting by
Ford Madox Brown, from
Birmingham Museum & Art Gallery,
Chamberlain Square,
Birmingham B3 3DH

Age
9–11

Purposes
● To raise awareness of how people feel when they leave their homeland.
● To recognise that history concerns ordinary people as well as the famous.

Activities
1 Circulate as many postcards as you have of the famous painting, *The Last of England*. Talk about it. Ask: *Does the picture give an idea about what is happening? Can they guess? How do they think the couple feel?* Then tell them that the painting depicts a couple emigrating to Australia in 1852.

2 In groups, they create the roles of other families on board the ship in 1852. Decide on a family name, the possessions being taken and the reason for leaving Britain to start a new life in Australia. Then create a **still image** of the family on board ship on the day of departure.

3 Talk about what conditions might have been like on board: *Was there sufficient food? Was the ship clean and sanitary? Was there a doctor and medicines?* Create a second still image showing the same family six weeks into the voyage.

4 The children create a still image entitled The First of Australia, coming into the picture one by one after deciding their role. **Bring** it **to life** for a few minutes.

Further activities
► Individually, the children write a dairy of their voyage.

► The whole class creates a performance poem on the theme of The Last of England. They are family and friends who are left behind as the emigrants leave. The poem's refrain is: 'They've seen the last of England. We've said our last good-byes.' Individuals create the lines preceding the refrain. They express ideas and feelings about their memories, the sadness they feel, what awaits the emigrants in a new land, fears about the voyage.

68 When the railway came

Drama space
Classroom or hall

Organisation
The class split in half,
then smaller groups

Resources
Materials for making posters and
placards; megaphones made of card

Age
9–11

pcm 68 on page 84

Purpose

● To explore part of History Study Unit
3a, Victorian Britain: the growth of
railways and the impact of railways on
everyday life.

Activities

1 Provide everyone with a copy of pcm
68. Read the two texts together and
discuss the issues they raise. You may
need to spend some time over the
archaic phraseology. Explain that the
building of the railways caused much
controversy in the mid-19th century and
that the text is based upon actual
documents of the time.

2 Divide the class in half, one half
representing the protesters and the other
the supporters. Each group declaims the
appropriate text or a portion of it with as
much drama as possible. This could
include solo voices, pairs and the full
group. There is no action required as it is
the power of the language that is
important. Ask each group to present
their dramatic reading.

3 In smaller groups within the two
halves, the children design and produce
posters and placards with slogans
supporting their case.

4 Working in small groups, the children
create short **scenes**, called *When the
Railway Came*. They may use the text,
their posters, placards, and megaphones
made out of card. The scenes might
depict such themes as: railway accidents;
people losing all their savings when
railway companies become bankrupt;
tourists enjoying the scenery from the
train; an emergency visit to family far
away. Show the scenes.

Further activity

► Present the two scenes in assembly or
to a small invited audience.

69 Thomas More

Drama space
Classroom

 Subject link
RE

Organisation
Whole class, small groups, individuals

Resources
Chairs in a circle; a bible or similar
large book; paper crown or sceptre

Age
9–11

pcm 69 on page 85

Purposes

● To consider life in Tudor times.
● To learn about Thomas More's role in
history.

Activities

1 Hand out pcm 69 to everyone. Read it
and discuss the issues raised.

2 Each child sits on their own chair in a
circle. Say that the space in the middle is
Thomas More's prison cell and ask them
to each describe the cell as they imagine
it in a word or short phrase.

3 In small groups, the children create
still pictures of moments in Thomas
More's life, some of the groups depicting
him before imprisonment and some
after. The moments could be with his
family, with the king, with a prison guard,
at his studies.

4 Place an object, such as a paper crown
or sceptre, on one of the chairs to
represent Henry VIII. Each child takes it
in turn to plead with the king for More's
life, standing in front of the chair.
Remind them to be persuasive.

5 Slowly, one by one, the children
approach the king's chair from behind
and pause. This time each one speaks
Henry VIII's thoughts. They do not say
what the king has decided, but only what
he is thinking.

6 Place a book representing a bible on
another chair as Thomas, who has heard
that he is to be executed. Repeat the
action in step 5, this time having each
child speak the thoughts of Thomas.

70 Wreckers

Drama space
Hall

Subject links

PSHE, RE

Organisation
Small groups, whole class

Age
9–11

Note
You will need only enough copies of the pcm for those participating in step 6 as wreckers and officers.

pcm 70 on page 86

Purposes
● To examine the morality of smuggling and shipwrecking in past times in the light of great poverty.

Activities
1 Using a few simple **props**, such as chairs or PE benches, ask the children in small groups to create a part of a sailing ship: a passenger cabin, the sailor's quarters, part of the deck, for example. Each group shows the rest of the class what they have created. Talk about conditions and the way of life on board ship. Then ask the groups to devise a short **scene** in the part of the ship they have created. The time is as the ship is close to home after a long voyage.

2 Using a different part of the space, enact a drama in which a wrecking gang is being recruited. Use the details on pcm 7044 to give the background of the people who are being recruited. Take the role of the recruitment agent. Each child should make their own decision about whether to join the gang or not.

3 In a circle facing *inwards*, each child in turn speaks the thoughts or tiny fragments of conversation of the passengers and crew of the sailing ship.

Remind them that they do not know there are wreckers about. Then all face *outwards* in the circle and speak the thoughts of the wreckers. Repeat the inwards and outwards thoughts a couple of times to build tension.

4 The group return to the part of the ship they created earlier and rearrange it as though it had been wrecked.

5 Imagine the wreckers have been caught and brought to court for trial. The class organises their trial, agreeing what punishment is to be given if the wreckers are found guilty. Give some guidance as to what punishments were likely in the historical period.

6 Conduct the trial with as many of the following as is feasible: judge, customs and excise officers, survivors, crew, wreckers, families of the wreckers, prosecution and defence solicitors. Hand out pcm 70 to the individuals or groups playing the wreckers and the custom and excise officers to be used for background or actual speeches.

7 Discuss the sort of punishment that might be meted out today in the light of current morality.

71 Aztecs

Drama space
Hall

Background
Some knowledge of the Aztecs and their culture

Organisation
Various sized groups

Age
9–11

Purpose
● To explore aspects of other cultures, particularly the Aztecs.

Activities
1 In groups of four, the children invent Aztec names for each other. Remind them that names were different for boys and girls. Angry Eagle, Leaping Puma, Stone Face were boys' names, for example; Green Jade, Laughing Water, Rain Bird, were girls' names. If they can, children should choose names that in some way reflect a particular character trait, or one they might like to have, for each group member.

2 In groups of about six, the children think of different jobs that might need doing around an Aztec home. (This may need further research.) Ask them to create a **still picture** in which they do one of the jobs, then **bring** the picture **to life**.

3 Discuss what they think of the way in which boys and girls were brought up to perform different jobs.

4 In groups of four, three are traders from other parts of the Aztec empire and one is the Aztec collecting tribute from them, as was the law. The traders have either hidden their wealth or are prepared to lie about it in order to avoid paying the tribute.

5 Split the class in half; one group **role plays** traders selling such merchandise as maize, chillies, beans, cloth, featherwork, pottery, metal goods and possibly even slaves. The other group are the buyers. They need to decide what they are looking for and what goods or food they are prepared to barter.

72 Evacuees

Drama space
Classroom or hall

Organisation
Whole class, pairs, groups of 4

Resources
Blackboard or flip chart

Age
9–11

pcm 72 on page 87

Purposes

● To bring to life a period in 20th-century wartime history.

● To examine the emotional impact evacuation made on children of their own age.

Activities

1 Give each child a copy of pcm 72 and read aloud the postcard.

2 Ask the children to imagine that they are about to be evacuated. Brainstorm words which describe how they think they would feel. Write these words on a blackboard or flip chart for reference, dividing them into positive and negative emotions.

3 In pairs, ask the children to create two **still pictures**, the first showing a parent and child saying good-bye, the second

showing something of the new life described in the postcard. Share these images.

4 In groups of about four, ask the children to enact a **scene** showing the first meeting between the evacuated child and their new family. Encourage the children to think about how each individual reacts at this first meeting.

5 Each child sits in a space of their own with eyes closed. Ask them to imagine that they are in their new bedroom on the first night away from home. Encourage them to think about how they feel. Say that when you tap each of them on the shoulder, you want them to say just briefly how they are feeling. They keep their eyes closed.

6 Ask each child to write their own postcard home after a few days away.

73 Pandora's box

Drama space
Classroom or hall

Subject link
RE

Organisation
Whole class, pairs, 7 groups

Resources
Any version of *Pandora's Box*; paper and pens; musical instruments optional

Age
9–11

Purposes

● To dramatise a story from Greek Mythology as part of a larger history project on the Ancient Greeks.

● To explore creation stories.

Activities

1 Read the story of *Pandora's box*.

2 Discuss with the class how you could break the story into seven sections, using the headings below as your own guide.

Suggested headings

1 People are happy and carefree.

2 The gods create Pandora.

3 Zeus gives Pandora the box.

4 Pandora and Epimetheus meet and marry.

5 Epimetheus hides the box.

6 Pandora opens the box and all the evil things escape.

7 Hope flies into the world.

3 In pairs, ask the class to draw a comic strip of the story with eight pictures, one for each section of the story and a title frame. Each picture should have one short line of text underneath describing the action.

4 Split the class into seven groups and give each group one section of the story. Ask them to create a **still picture** of that section and create a line of text, like those in the comic strip, to be spoken before the picture is shown.

5 Show the still pictures in the correct order so that the whole story is told.

Further activities

► Develop this work:

– Add a percussion element to the still picture, using either instruments, the children's voices, clapping or a combination of these.

– Ask the groups to develop three still pictures, instead of one, for their sections. Develop the still images into **mimed scenes** by **bringing** each scene **to life** and, with as little movement as possible, changing from scene to scene in sequence. Keep the movements simple, slow and clear.

74 Off with her head!

Drama space
Classroom or hall

Organisation
Whole class, small groups

Resources
Any picture of Anne Boleyn

Age
9–11

Purposes

● To begin to gain an understanding of the human consequences of Henry VIII's actions.

● To explore the feelings and emotions of his most famous wife.

Activities

1 Show the class the picture of Anne Boleyn and talk about her life (see below). Talk about why Henry was so keen to have a son rather than a daughter. In small groups, the children create two short **scenes**. The first shows how Anne thought King Henry would respond to the news that she had given birth to a baby daughter. The second shows how the group think he actually did respond.

2 Choose a class member, or use pictures of a crown and royal dress of Henry's period, to represent Anne Boleyn in her cell in the Tower of London on 18 May 1536. It is the eve of her execution. In a circle around Anne, the children take it in turns to speak her thoughts. Develop this by feeding in Anne's very different feelings on first hearing that Henry wanted to marry her.

> **Anne Boleyn** (1507 – 1536) was the second and most famous of the six wives of **Henry VIII**. Anne was a maid of honour to **Catherine of Aragon**, Henry VIII's first wife, when Henry became interested in her. She was only 18 years old and very lively and clever. Henry married Anne in January 1533 while there was still a lot of confusion about the divorce from Catherine. She was crowned queen in June and gave birth to a girl, **Elizabeth**, in September. Anne became a power at court and used her power harshly. She was proud and domineering, making many enemies.
>
> When Anne had failed to produce a son after three years, Henry wanted to get rid of her. He was already interested in another young woman at court and was tired of Anne. Henry had her condemned to death and beheaded at the Tower of London on 19 May 1536. It is said that she died with dignity. Henry married **Jane Seymour** the day after Anne's execution.

75 Remembrance

Drama space
Classroom

Subject link
RE

Organisation
Whole class, small groups

Age
9–11

Note
This is appropriate for use near or on Poppy Day.

Purposes

● To explore the idea of remembering those who have died, particularly related to veterans of war and Poppy Day.

Activities

1 Discuss Poppy Day and its significance. *Do the children have any relatives who have died fighting in wars? Why do people honour those who were killed in combat? Should we still do so? For how long should these acts of remembrance continue?*

2 Read some war poems.

3 Working in small groups, the children create a **still picture** called The Eve of Battle. Some groups are soldiers at the front, some are people at home. In each picture, there can be a mixture of people involved in different tasks. Show the still images one by one, asking the participants in turn to speak their thoughts aloud.

4 The groups create new still pictures showing the same people after a battle. Some soldiers will be dead, others injured. Some people at home may be getting bad news about their loved ones. The living speak their thoughts first, then if the children can handle the dramatic licence, the dead speak. Was the sacrifice justified? What do the living owe the dead?

Further activities

▶ Invite a local vicar, priest or minister to tell the class about the type of rememberance services their church holds.

▶ Invite a veteran or a representative from a veteran's organisation to speak to the class about wartime experiences.

76 Chinese New Year

Drama space
Hall

Organisation
Whole class or 10 groups

Resources
Taped Chinese music if possible

Age
5–7

Purposes
● To understand in more detail one aspect of the Chinese New Year.
● To develop imaginative movement skills.

Activities
1 Read aloud the story below and make sure the children understand it.

2 Ask the children to find a space and then talk about the first animal, the tiger. Ask for the children's ideas on how a tiger moves and then let them move around like a tiger. Suggest that they don't have to walk on all fours, but just use their bodies in tiger-like movements.

3 Work through all the animals in this way, using Chinese music as background if possible. If appropriate, ask the children to create sounds for each animal.

4 **Narrate** the story as the children enact it. Some children could be the gods and could also watch the race. For the race itself, encourage slow motion movement using the ideas developed in step 2. The scene breakdown (bottom) can be used as a guide. Your narration should lead the children carefully through each stage of the story.

5 If you prefer, you could divide the class into 10 groups, create a **still image** for each **scene** and then gradually add movement and dialogue to tell the whole story.

Many years ago in China the years had no names or numbers. People grew tired of this, so they went to talk to the gods. This is what they always did when they had a problem. The gods came up with a very good idea. 'Why don't you name the years after the animals?' The people were very pleased with this idea. So were the animals, but straightaway they started arguing.

'I should be first,' said the tiger. 'My stripes are so smart and I am so handsome and elegant.'

'No. I should be first,' retorted the monkey. 'I'm by far the cleverest animal.'

'But I do the most work and am stronger than you all,' said the ox.

'But I run fastest,' said the horse.

'People love me best,' said the dog. 'I am a loyal friend.'

'But you can't give milk and warm clothes like I can,' replied the goat.

'I am the most gracessssssful and the quietesssssst,' hissed the snake.

'But none of you can compare to my fierceness and beauty,' roared the dragon.

'I run fastest and burrow the best,' put in the rabbit.

'Speed isn't everything. I take my time over things,' said the boar.

And the rat listened to them all and chuckled.

So the gods decided there should be a race, and the order in which the animals reached the goal would be the order in which the years were named. The first part of the race was through a thick dark forest. The second part was over a muddy rice field. Finally the animals had to swim across the river to the far bank.

As they approached the bank, the ox was ahead. But just before it reached the bank, the crafty rat leapt off the ox's back where it had hidden and reached the shore first. So the first year was named after the rat. The other years in order were: ox, tiger, rabbit, dragon, snake, horse, goat, monkey, rooster, dog, pig.

Just then the lion came bounding up. It had been asleep and had not heard about the race. To make up for its disappointment, the gods decided that the lion should lead the New Year procession every year.

Scene Breakdown

1 Village scene: villagers attempt to talk about the past, showing the problem without names or numbers for years.

2 The villagers and the gods discuss the problem and the gods come up with an idea.

3 The animals argue about which should be the first year.

4 The race is announced.

5 The race through the forest.

6 The race across the rice field.

7 The race across the river.

8 The rat cheats and wins. The other animals are angry.

9 The gods announce the order of the years.

10 The lion arrives late. The gods give it something to do.

77 Journey to Bethlehem

Drama space
Hall

Organisation
Whole class, small groups

Resources
A bible would be useful

Age
7–9

 pcm 77 on page 88

Purpose
● To think about the serious side of Christmas.

Activities
1 Tell the class that this drama will be about Joseph and Mary's journey to Bethlehem but from an unusual angle. You might first wish to read relevant extracts from the bible.

2 Ask the children to imagine that they are living at the time of Joseph and Mary and have to travel to Bethlehem to register. This may be a very long journey with none of the modern ease of travel. Ask them to sit in a place by themselves and imagine the kind of journey they might have. **Narrate** some ideas with questions or descriptions about the conditions along the way. Ask each child to describe their imagined journey to one other child.

3 Give out pcm 77 and explain the blank identity cards. Ask the children to work in small groups which will be a family. The group should decide upon a fictional identity conforming to each item on the identity card and including the adults

and children. No one should take the names of Joseph or Mary. Everyone should complete their identity card, each one drawing a picture of themselves. (Remind them to draw clothing appropriate to the biblical period.)

4 Tell them each person is allowed to take only three items on the journey, and will have to carry them a long way alone. Ask the children to **mime** packing the three items.

5 Ask each group to decide on a moment of danger on the journey. This could be an accident, illness, attack by bandits, for example. Each group shows that moment by making a **still picture**.

6 Put up a barrier to represent the border. You are now **in role** as a Roman official. You look at all identity cards and question each traveller closely.

7 Sit in a circle. The children imagine they saw the infant Jesus in Bethlehem as they entered the city. Go round the circle giving each child the chance to offer a very brief description of what they saw or heard.

78 An Icelandic legend

Drama space
Classroom and hall

Organisation
Whole class, then small groups

Resources
Tape recorder; lengths of cloth and percussion instruments would be useful

Age
7–11

 pcm 78 on page 89

Purpose
● To use creation myths as a way of thinking about comparative religions.

Activities
1 Explain the word 'myth'. Provide each child with a copy of pcm 78. Working line by line or any alternative method, ask the children to read aloud: one line by an individual, one by a pair, one by a small group, one by the whole class (or your own arrangement). Try to elicit a sensitive response to the rhythm of the language. Use a tape recorder and play back.

2 Discuss the striking images of the myth, perhaps comparing them to the Native American version on pcm 79. What are some of the differences? Are there similarities?

3 Give the class time to experiment with the various sounds of the piece: the icy

rivers, the fountain bursting forth, the fire meeting the ice rivers, the creation of Yamir and the world. Use voices and/or percussion instruments.

4 Work on a **movement sequence** in groups on two themes: some groups create the land of fire in the south. Others create land of ice in the north. The groups should try to represent the very different atmospheres of these two places. Then use slow motion action to express the part of the myth where the two lands come together. Read the details of the text again before you begin this.

Further activities
▶ Put the choral and spoken elements together with the movement sequences to create a performance for assembly or an invited audience.

79 A Native American myth

Drama space
Hall

Organisation
Whole class, small groups

Resources
Tape recorder; percussion instruments would be useful

Age
7–11

pcm 79 on page 90

Purpose
● To use creation myths as a way of thinking about comparative religions.

Activities
1 Explain the word 'myth'. Provide each child with a copy of pcm 79. Working line by line or any alternative method, ask the children to read aloud: one line by an individual, one by a pair, one by a small group, one by the whole class (or your own arrangement). Try to elicit a sensitive response to the rhythm of the language. Use a tape recorder and play back.

2 Discuss the striking images of the myth. Ask the children what the myth tells them about Native Americans.

3 Give the class time to experiment with the various sounds of the piece: the wind, the thunder and lightening, the pebble dropping, rivers flowing. Use voices and/or percussion instruments.

4 Work on key moments of the story through movement. Create the various forces with the help of different kinds of posture, different speeds, and stillness and action. In small groups, one child could create movement for the clouds, another the winds, another the lightening and another the thunder. The groups could choose appropriate music with your help or make their own sounds.

Further activities
► Using movement, voice and sound, perform the key movements in assembly or to an invited audience.

80 The Trimurti

Drama space
Hall

Organisation
Whole class

Resources
Drum or tambourine

Age
9–11

pcm 80 on page 91

Purpose
● To raise awareness of an aspect of the Hindu culture.

Activities
1 Explain the word 'myth'. Provide each child with a copy of pcm 80. Working line by line or any alternative method, ask the children to read aloud: one line by an individual, one by a pair, one by a small group, one by the whole class (or your own arrangement). Discuss the similarities and differences between this and other creation stories the children know.

2 Discuss the three parts of the Trimurti. Ask the children to find a space and take up a pose to represent in turn Brahma, Vishnu, and Shiva, as you give a **signal** to change. Remind them of the specific jobs of each.

3 Read again the part of the story where the animals come out of Brahma. Ask each child to choose an animal, bird or insect and move slowly around the room in the way they think that creature would move.

4 Give each child a number. Ask them all to create one huge shape in the centre of the room to represent Brahma. As you call out each number, that child should come slowly out of Brahma and move around the room as the creature they chose in step 3. Continue until all are out of Brahma.

81 The meeting

Drama space
Hall

Subject link
Geography

Organisation
Whole class split in half

Resources
Tape or ropes

Age
7–9

Purpose

● To explore how to meet, communicate with and respect different cultures, without a shared language.

Activities

1 Split the class in half, naming one half the Farmers and the other half the Nomads. Explain that you are going to use the space in a special way. The large central area, marked with tape or ropes, is the meeting ground and field of Farmers, while spaces at each end are the home base for each group. The Farmers are working there one day when the Nomads arrive. Neither group have ever met before and do not share a language. Explain that the drama depends on everyone observing the following rules:
1) No one is to talk in the central area.
2) They can only communicate by signs.
3) If either group wishes to discuss something, they must go to their home base to talk. 4) The groups are not allowed to visit each other's home bases.

2 Talk to each group privately, giving the following information:

Farmers

This year there is a rich harvest and they need extra help. They have a spring which gives plenty of water, but they are not good potters and find it hard to make drinking cups.

Nomads

They need food and water. They have travelled a long way. They are skilled at making simple but strong pottery. They make it in one place at the start of each year and carry a supply with them wherever they go.

3 Start the drama and let it take its course.

82 The tower of Babel

Drama space
Hall

Subject link
PSHE

Organisation
Small groups, whole class

Resources
Bible in modern translation

Age
9–11

Purpose

● To think about the value of learning from stories.
● To explore a bible story.

Activities:

1 Read aloud the story of the Tower of Babel from Genesis, Chapter 11. In small groups, the children choose a leader. This leader has already decided where to live and build the tower and is going to announce the decision at an important general **meeting**. He or she needs help with this very important speech. The speech needs to give the reason for the tower, an idea of its size and the fact that it will involve hard work. Each group plans the speech to convince everyone to accept the leader's decision. The class listens to some of the finished speeches.

2 **Narrate solo movement** in which the workers struggle with the heavy blocks of stone as they build the tower. Freeze the movement and allow the workers to speak their thoughts. Do they really think the tower is a good idea?

3 In a circle, **in role**, they stand at the base of the tower that stretches up and up into the sky. The leader announces that only he or she is allowed to go to the top. The others speak words or phrases that describe how they feel. What do they think it is like at the top? Do they want to go up? Do they think it is fair that only the leader can go?

4 Create the storm in a series of whole-class **still pictures** which show the reaction of the crowd as the storm grows and the tower begins to sway. Then everyone lies on the floor.

5 Narrate that the tower has been destroyed. Slowly people stand up and begin to move about looking at the devastation. Individuals speak, but no one understands them. Confusion begins to spread. **Freeze** to create a whole-class still picture.

Further activities

► As a class, think about times in today's world when communication seems to break down, either through technical failure or unwillingness to listen to each other.

83 Journeys

Drama space
Hall

Organisation
Whole class; small groups or pairs
optional in step 4

Resources
Pencils; paper for each child or a single
large sheet of paper (see step 4); mats;
small hoops

Age
7–9

Purpose

● To familiarise children with basic geographical and spatial concepts.

Activities

1 In the hall or other large space, play Spaceship Squad or the better known variant, Captain's Coming. Choose different walls of the space to be the engine room, dining room, observatory and bridge. When you call out these names, the children are to run to that area. When you call 'red alert', they must sit down on the floor wherever they are and **mime** putting on their seat belt. If you call 'spacecraft commander', they stand where they are and salute.

2 Sit down in one large group and explain that the starship has landed on a new planet which they are to explore. Set some parameters before you start, such as no fights with aliens. Explain the geography of the planet as revealed by the spaceship sensors, stressing that it contains no animals or creatures but has an abundance of trees and plants. Go on to explain some of the geographical features such as woods, mountains and rivers. Set off on a journey together to explore the planet, with you **in role** as leader, going over hills, through ditches and so on.

3 **Out of role**, say that later there will be a reporting session in which you require absolute accuracy for the spaceship records. *Where did you go on your journey and what did you see?* Use geographical and spatial terms and reinforce the importance of describing the journey as a sequence of events.

4 Explain that the records must contain plans, maps and pictures or photographs of the journey. The exact terminology you use will depend on the age of the class and their familiarity with these concepts. Back in role you could work as a whole group on one large sheet of paper with you drawing the route and children adding their own pictures. Or you could send them off in small groups or pairs to work on their own. The aim is to begin to work out how to translate a physical journey onto paper.

5 Still in role, everyone helps to set up camp around the spaceship, using chairs and PE equipment to make four areas: food store, meeting area, equipment area, spaceship entrance. Place mats across the room to represent a river dividing the camp, and place small hoops at one point to denote stepping stones.

6 Enact ordinary life in the camp, undertaking such tasks as cleaning and preparing food, holding planning meetings, eating together, setting up equipment, maintaining the spaceship. After a while, bring everyone together and report that the stepping stones are starting to sink because of so much use. *How will you deal with this situation?* As leader, make some suggestions. (See below.) Then discuss them and agree on an option.

Some possible choices are:

– for everyone to plan their work carefully so that they cross the river as little as possible

– to allow only a certain number of journeys across the river each day, enforced by posting guards on the stones

– to redesign the camp so that it is all on one side of the river

– to find a new way of crossing the river.

84 All aboard!

Drama space
Hall

Organisation
Groups, then the class split
into two groups optional

 Subject link
PSHE

Background
Some knowledge of life aboard
an ocean-going ship, through pictures
and discussion

Age
7–11

Purpose
● To help reflect on the plight of refugees.

Activities
1 Define an area to represent the gangplank of an ocean liner. Each child is to go aboard for a pleasure cruise, carrying heavy bags up a narrow, wobbly gangway. Then they have to find their cabin, asking help from passers-by.

2 In groups, they show a **still picture** of activity in one part of the ship. It could be working in the engine room, eating in the dining room, playing games on the deck, for example. Each child chooses a **role** in the still image so that, when they are asked, they can **bring** the picture **to life**.

3 Then say that a big storm has blown up and it is very difficult to move about the ship. Ask them to move and sway as the ship rolls and rocks in the storm.

4 The evening of the Captain's Dinner arrives and everyone moves around the room getting to know each other. The captain circulates to keep things going. (You may wish to take the role of captain.)

5 The cruise is over. The passengers pack their bags. Then they move carefully down the narrow gangway to disembark. Encourage an atmosphere of friendly leave-taking.

6 Explain that they are now going to enact a drama on the same ship but this time as people whose lives are under threat in their own country. In order to escape, they are illegal stowaways hiding below decks. The activities now become:
– sneaking aboard and finding a place to hide
– still pictures of trying to sleep, stealing food, trying to get fresh air, keeping out of sight
– enduring a fearful storm in the cramped conditions in the hideaway
– evading a search party
– sneaking ashore in what they hope is a friendly country.

Further activities
► To create a whole drama, you could split the class into two with one half enacting the pleasure cruise and the other the voyage of the refugees. As one group **freezes**, the other takes up the story.

85 Erosion

Drama space
Classroom or hall

Organisation
Whole class, pairs, small groups

Resources
A portable tape recorder or
video camera would be useful

Age
9–11

Purpose
● To explore how people affect the environment in relation to the causes of coastal erosion.

Activities
1 Tell the children that you read a newspaper story about a house, built on a cliff, falling into the sea. The home owners claim that the collapse was caused by the construction of new sea defences further along the coast. They say that the new wall has changed the force of the waves and this, in turn, eroded the cliff. The family is now homeless and very upset. The local council insists that there is no scientific evidence to support the family's claim.

2 In small groups, the children devise short **scenes** showing the plight of the family whose house collapsed. They could present: moments of fear as early cracks start to appear in the walls; the actual collapse; the family leaving; trying

to salvage a few of their belongings.

3 The whole class plans, rehearses and presents a TV news item about the incident. The following roles are needed:
– The programme presenter(s)
– The audience
– The family whose home collapsed.
– Expert scientist(s) who can give evidence about erosion and cliffs slipping into the sea.
– Builders who were involved in constructing the new sea defences.
– Local people who can give evidence about the changing conditions in the area.
– Camera operators. (An actual video camera would be very useful.)

At the end of the programme, ask the audience for their opinions. Then take a vote on whether or not they believed the collapse was caused by the building of the sea defences.

86 Land use

Drama space
Classroom

Resources
Coloured felt-tip pens

Organisation
Groups of 4, then 4 groups

Age
9–11

Note
You need only enough copies of the pcm for one shared by four.

pcm 86 on page 92

Purpose
● To explore aspects of the use of land and the issues this raises.

Activities
1 In groups of four, hand out copies of pcm 86. The children use different colours to identify on the map: the town wall remains, the leisure centre, the school and the shopping centre.

2 Offer these three possible uses for the waste ground:

– Leave it as it is since it contains part of the medieval town wall. Although the wall is much better preserved elsewhere, and the section crossing the wasteland is only a track with a few scattered stones, the Old Town Preservation Society is in favour of this option.

– Expand the shopping centre. The shopping centre management proposed this option and will buy the land.

– Build a new leisure centre on it. The leisure centre is in a very poor state of repair and its open-air swimming pool can only be used during the summer for school swimming lessons. It is far from the school. The leisure centre management and the school favour building a new centre on the waste ground.

3 Split the class into four groups. Three groups represent the above factions; the fourth is the town council which must sanction any change of use for the land. Allow the interest groups time to prepare their arguments, while the council group sets up the **meeting** space and decides how the meeting will be run. They should also study the issues in readiness for the meeting.

4 Hold the council meeting, allowing each group to present their case. The council members and the other group members ask questions. Then the council retires to reach a decision.

87 Light and dark

Drama space
Hall

Subject link
RE

Organisation
Individuals, whole class

Resources
Large sheet of paper and felt-tip pens or large crayons

Age
5–9

Purpose
● To use an imaginary journey to extend vocabulary around the theme.

Activities
1 Settle the class in the hall and explain that you are all going on an imaginary journey which is so long that you have to set off before daybreak. Move into the drama by asking the children to imagine that they are getting up and dressing while it is still dark. They work individually, each in their own space, to your **narration**, **miming** as you speak. Explain that they should get dressed quietly by the dim light of a torch so that they don't wake everyone else. Encourage movement which reflects the care and slight fumbling that occurs due to tiredness and poor light. Narrate them out through their front door (closed quietly) and into the street.

2 Continue the narration to take the children out into the countryside. In keeping with the theme, use light-related words: pools of light from the street lamps, a flickering advertising sign, shining car headlamps, the pre-dawn glow in the sky, the pale early sun...

3 Lead them through fields and woodland and stop outside a cave. Ask the children to peer in and describe what they can see.

4 Take the children into the cave. Narrate how they stop once they are inside to get their eyes used to the dark,

and how they switch on torches as they continue their journey. Look for opportunities to use light- and dark-related words: pitch dark, shaft of light, glittering stones, shimmering water, inky blackness...

5 When you have reached the heart of the cave, gather everyone around your bright light and explain that you are going to leave something here for anyone else who comes this way to find. Unroll your large sheet of paper and ask four children to hold the corners down. Draw, or have drawn already, a long wiggly line representing the journey. You can mark the edge of town, the cave mouth, and the heart of the cave where you are now. Ask the children to use light and dark words to tell you about the journey. As they do so, write the words on the sheet. You might end up with words such as: dark house, bright torch, pools of light, sunrise, pale light, dark cave, and so on.

6 Lead everyone out of the cave, encouraging them to squint and blink in the bright sun after the dark.

Further activities
► The map that you produced can be used as an aid for further description of the journey or for writing Light and Dark poems, perhaps accompanied by artwork.

88 Dinosaurs

Drama space
Hall

Subject link
Dance

Organisation
Whole class, pairs, group of 5

Resources
Taped music for slow movement would be helpful

Background
Knowledge of dinosaurs and their names

Age
5–9

Purposes
● To use children's interest in dinosaurs as a stimulus for drama.
● To develop controlled movements.

Activities
1 Read the story (right) to the class and ask them which parts they found most exciting.
2 Ask the children to spread out and stand in a space of their own.
3 Ask for suggestions on how they think the Tyrannosaurus would move. When you have enough suggestions, ask them to move around the room like a Tyrannosaurus but in slow motion. (Music would be helpful at this point.)
4 Talk about the Stegosaurus. Encourage the children to think about how they could create the spiked tail. Suggest they work in pairs to create one Stegosaurus.
5 In groups of about five, ask the children to re-create the final battle, using the movement ideas they have practised and keeping the whole scene in slow motion. Tell the children that they should not actually touch each other at any time but should find other ways of showing that Tyrannosaurus is biting, being lashed with a tail, and so on.

A great **Tyrannosaurus Rex** is searching for a meal. The huge dinosaur's appetite is never satisfied and today it is very hungry. Its giant legs crash down on the land, sending other creatures rushing for shelter. Its huge teeth flash in the sun.

Suddenly the king of the dinosaurs spies a young **Stegosaurus** drinking from a pool. The great beast is upon its prey in an instant, sinking sharp teeth into the smaller dinosaur's neck. The giant hits bony plates and looses its grip for a moment. The Stegosaurus seizes its chance and slams its heavy, spiked tail into the side of its attacker. The Tyrannosaurus roars in anger and pain, but turns to finish the job with its fearsome jaws open. Now the terrified shrieks of the younger creature brings the rest of the herd to its rescue. They lash the giant dinosaur with their spiked tails just as it is about to bite its prey again. The Tyrannosaurus fights back and draws blood from many of the Stegosaurus. But it is outnumbered and retreats to nurse its wounds.

Today the Tyrannosaurus will not have a meal of Stegosaurus. But the spiky-tailed dinosaurs know that it will return another day.

89 Dolphin Park

Drama space
Classroom

Subject link
PSHE

Organisation
Individuals, whole class

Age
5–7

Purpose
● To raise issues related to caring for animals.

Activities
1 Read the notice below and discuss it, ensuring that the class understands the concept of a special water park for dolphins.

Ladies and gentlemen

I am pleased to announce the opening of Dolphin Park here in your community. Our three beautiful dolphins have come all the way from the Atlantic Ocean to perform tricks just for you.

The park opens this Saturday. It's free for this weekend only, so don't miss it.

2 Working individually or in pairs, they make posters for the park.
3 Working individually, they imagine that it is the night before the park opens. What are the dolphins thinking? Ask some children to speak one of the dolphin's thoughts aloud. Try to elicit excitement at doing the tricks, fear of appearing before an audience, sadness at being parted from their natural home.
4 The class have the chance to meet with the owner of the Dolphin Park. What will the children say? Help them make a list of questions that explore the lives of the dolphins both in the wild and in captivity. **In role** as the owner, enact the **meeting**.

90 Space race

Drama space
Hall

Subject link
PSHE

Organisation
Whole class, groups of 4 or 5,
class split in half

Age
7–11

Purpose
● To raise awareness of the Apollo programme and some of its implications.

Activities
1 Begin with a class discussion about the Apollo programme. Find out what the children know about how the Americans landed on the moon. Introduce any or all of the following: contemporary newspaper cuttings, non-fiction books and CD-ROMs.

2 In the drama space, tell the children that a Wagon Train of poor people arrived at Cape Kennedy at the time of the Apollo 11 launch. These people wished the astronauts no harm but questioned why so much money was being spent on the moon programme when great need existed in the country. Discuss the experience of poverty: no work, no medical insurance, no holidays, no heat, for example. In groups of four or five, ask the children to create **still pictures** showing a life of poverty. Share and discuss these in turn, as a class.

3 **Narrate** the following actions or use your own version.

> You are an astronaut in training for a mission to the moon and you must be physically fit. Do sit ups until I say stop… Now jog around to warm up for the morning's training session… Put on your space suit and connect all the hoses and sensors.
>
> Now I want you to show me still pictures of your busy day. Make each still picture as I describe it.
>
> – You are sitting in the simulator at the controls learning to fly the spacecraft.
>
> – You are experiencing heavy G forces and feeling like you weigh ten times your normal weight.
>
> – You are opening the door of the simulator to go out into space.
>
> – It's lunch time, so you take off your space suit and eat.
>
> – You watch the building of the rocket that will thrust you into space.
>
> – You are back in the simulator at the controls.
>
> – You receive a phone call. Freeze.

This is what you hear:

> 'Gus Grissom, Ed White and Roger Chaffee have died in a terrible fire on the launch pad. They had spent long hours in their Apollo spacecraft in a full rehearsal for the blast off. Suddenly one of them saw a flame. They radioed for help, but it was too late. Their only escape route was the hatch, which would take two minutes to open. But it was only seconds before the temperature rose so high that the astronauts stood no chance of survival. They died, poisoned by toxic fumes, before anyone could get to them.'

Freeze the action at the end of the narration and ask a few children to speak their thoughts out loud as astronauts who have just heard of the deaths (**thought tracking**).

4 Split the class in half. One group acts as members of the poverty Wagon Train, the other as astronauts and NASA personnel. It is the day of the Apollo 11 launch. The two sides meet. What do they say to each other? Suggest that the NASA staff remember all their hard work over the years, and the death of their friends. The poor people want to know why the billions spent on the moon programme could not be spent on their needs. How do NASA staff justify the expenditure?

Further activities
► Split the class into five teams and give each team a topic for research:
1 the Saturn rockets
2 the first men on the moon
3 the other moon landings
4 Apollo 13
5 the space race between America and Russia.

Using the material they have researched, each team might present a short TV programme based on it.

91 Not just for Christmas

Drama space
Classroom or hall

Subject link
PSHE

Organisation
Whole class, groups of 4, small groups

Age
7–11

pcm 91 on page 93

Purposes
● To develop the skill of persuasive argument.
● To raise awareness of cruelty to animals.

Activities
1 In a circle, ask the children to name and describe as many different types of dog as they can. Try to decide what type of family and/or home each dog may suit.

2 In groups of four, two are **in role** as children who want a pet dog and two are parents who are reluctant to have one. The children try to persuade the parents to buy a dog. Stress that the children's arguments should be sensible and show that they will be responsible pet owners. Stop the **role play** and discuss the arguments put forward. Which were effective?

3 In small groups, using pcm 91, they think of some more questions they would ask in the survey.

4 Discuss what the children might do to prevent animals being mistreated in the areas of the school and their homes.

92 Energy and the environment

Drama space
Classroom or hall

Organisation
Groups of 3 or 4

Resources
Simple reference books on environmental issues.
The following books may be useful:

Captain Eco and The Fate of The Earth
Jonathon Porritt and Ellis Nadler
DK Publishers
ISBN 0 563 86318 703 X

The Young Person's Guide To Saving The Planet
Debbie Silver and Bernadette Vallely
Virago
ISBN 0 241 02234 7

The Blue Peter Green Book
BBC Books
ISBN 0 563 36330 4

Age
9–11

pcm 92 on page 94

Purposes
To raise awareness of the need to conserve energy and protect the environment.
To help young people think about positive action.

Activities
1 Give each child a copy of pcm 92 and discuss the issues raised.

2 In groups of three or four, ask the children to choose one specific issue.

Using books and their own experience and knowledge to explore this issue more deeply, they then decide on a message they would like to get across to other young people.

3 Each group creates a short TV advertisement of their message to appeal to young people of their own age. You could suggest the following format:

– Make a list of the points to get across.

– Produce a slogan, jingle, or such which expresses their message.

– Decide on the characters and the location for their advertisement.

– Work out how to enact it. (Each group could appoint a director.)

– Video the advertisements if your school has the facilities.

Further activities
► Present the TV advertisements at an assembly. To do this, add other visuals, such as posters, charts, photographs.

93 Paper Land

Drama space
Hall

Subject link
English

Resources
Large sheets of paper or newspaper;
thick pens or large crayons

Organisation
Whole class, pairs

Age
5–7

Purpose
● To provide an opportunity to combine drama with art.

Activities
1 Ask the class to imagine a land where everything is made of paper: the land itself and all the houses, trees, cars and so on. They should close their eyes for a few seconds to try to picture this strange land. When they open their eyes, share ideas together as a whole class.

2 Using large sheets of paper or newspaper, begin to create the objects in the land. Encourage the children to draw things as large as possible. Some shapes can lie flat on the floor, others can be taped upright to desks or chairs, others pinned to the wall, and so on.

3 Imagine you are all a group of earth people whose spacecraft has landed on the land of paper. In pairs, the children create **still pictures** showing their exploration of this unusual land. Each pair should work near one or more of the paper shapes, so creating a whole-class still image of the whole land being explored. **Freeze.**

4 **Bring** the exploration **to life** for a few moments, then freeze again.

5 Each pair reports back on what they found. Encourage them by asking: *Are there any paper people? Are they hiding? Are they frightened of us? Are they invisible?*

6 Continue the story through either drama, writing, drawing or discussion.

94 The story behind…

Drama space
Classroom or hall

Subject link
English

Organisation
Whole class, groups, individuals

Age
7–9

pcm 94A on page 95

pcm 94B on page 96

Purpose
● To become aware that a picture may have more than one interpretation.

Activities
1 In a circle, hand out copies of pcm 94A to each child and ask all to look at it in detail for 30 seconds. Go around the circle asking the children to say what they saw.

2 In groups, the children create a **still picture** which closely re-creates the image on the pcm.

3 Ask each group to **bring** their picture **to life** for a few seconds. Discuss the various intepretations of the picture revealed by this activity.

4 Ask individuals in turn to become the bystander and take the **hot seat**. The other children ask questions about what happened. If this activity needs support, you could take the role of the bystander. Try to come to an agreed interpretation or list several of the interpretations on the board.

5 Hand out pcm 94B. Ask some children for their reactions to it by putting them in the hot seat as either the girl, the teacher or the bystander.

6 Discuss how seeing the whole picture changes the interpretation of events.

95 Picture this...

Drama space
Classroom or hall

Subject link
English

Resources
Picture, photograph or magazine illustration with many characters in it (Lowrie painting, for example).

Organisation
Individuals, pairs

Age
7–11

Purpose
● To encourage care in interpreting artwork.

Activities
1 Working individually, the children re-create part of the selected painting or photograph as a **still picture** by choosing a **character** from it and adopting the character's position and pose.
2 Ask each to decide on a name and some background details for the character and to think about how they came to be in the picture. Ask individuals who have chosen the same character to work together and agree on the details for their character.
3 Ask the children in turn if they like the way they are shown in the picture. *If not, why? What would they change if they could?* They re-form the still picture with any changes they have agreed. Try **modelling** the still picture if it needs further improvement or change.
4 Now ask the children to think about what would happen immediately after the painting or photograph was completed. They create a still image and you **bring** it **to life**. Discuss.

96 Photo story

Drama space
Classroom, then where the action takes place

Subject link
English

Organisation
Groups of 7 or 8

Resources
Scrap paper; pencils or pens; white card or thick paper; one or more cameras; film (12 shots per group)

Age
9–11

Note
Step 5 will need to be staggered, depending on how many cameras are available.

Purposes
● To explore how dramatic photographs can tell a story.

Activities
1 In groups of seven or eight, give a choice of titles for a photo story, for example, *Stop thief!*, *Earthquake*, *The hypnotist*. Each group writes a short, simple story in keeping with the title. The **characters** should be four or five children of their own age.
2 Ask each group to divide their completed story into six sections and draw a simple sketch to illustrate the main action in each **scene**.
3 Ask each group to choose a director, photographer, designer and four or five actors.
4 Working from their six sketches, each group sets up six camera shots, one by one, using any simple props required. The director is responsible for arranging the actors in the best position to tell the story and making sure that their expressions are right. The designer finds the **props** and, if time permits, decides on any costumes.
5 The photographer sets up and takes each scene from the best angle, ensuring that everyone is in the picture. Two shots should be taken of each scene as a safeguard.
6 When the film has been developed, each group mounts their pictures in the story sequence and writes one or two lines of text or dialogue below each photograph.

97 Walking

Drama space
Hall

Organisation
Whole class

Age
5–7

Purpose
● To develop movement skills and encourage children to use their bodies imaginatively.

Activities
1 Ask the children to walk normally around the room either with bare feet or imagining they are barefoot. Then suggest different surfaces on which they are walking, for example, mud, hot sand, sharp rocks, ice, long grass. Encourage them to use their imaginations to alter the way they walk on the various surfaces.
2 Then ask them to imagine walking in different weather conditions as you

mention them: windy, very hot, pouring with rain, for example. They are still barefoot.
3 Next suggest obstacles they have to overcome: climbing steep steps, crawling through a tunnel, crossing a river on stepping stones.
4 Finally, tell them that they can have a rest. Ask them to decide what they are going to sit or lie on: a bench, soft grass, sand, perching on a wall. Their movements should show you what they have chosen.

 # 98 ABC

Drama space
Classroom or hall

 Subject link
English

Resources
Words below written in advance on blackboard or flip chart

Organisation
Whole class, groups of 3, pairs

Age
5–7

Purpose
● To develop movement and co-operation skills while improving basic literacy.

Activities
1 Explain that you are going to call out letters of the alphabet and that the children are going to create those letters using their whole body. Ask for a couple of volunteers and help them form two or three different lower case letters, taking ideas from the class as well.
2 With the children standing in their own space, call out some of the letters of the alphabet and ask them to create that letter. Letters such as x, d, h are better done in pairs or groups.

3 Form groups of four or five. Give each group a word from the blackboard, depending on whether it takes four or five to create it. Encourage the groups to form the letters in an upright position so the rest of the class can read the word easily.
4 When the words are completed, each group demonstrates their word for the rest of the class to read.
5 Depending on the age and ability of the children, you may wish to ask three groups to work together to create a short three word phrase or sentence, for example, the hot sun; the dog sat.
cat, dog, run, box, ant, log, big, top, can, hot, sky, sun, the

99 Above, below, behind, in front, beside!

Drama space
Hall

Resources
A bean bag or similar small soft object for each child

 Subject link
Geography

Organisation
Whole class

Age
5–7

Purpose
● To use drama to explore spacial concepts.

Activities
1 Ask each child to collect a bean bag, find a space, and do what you ask them to. Say: *Put the bean bag above you. Put the bean bag in front of you.* Say this sentence with all the words: below, behind, beside.

2 Speed the actions and say only the key word: 'above', 'below' and so on.

3 Change this into a game of Simon Says still using bean bags and key words.

4 Put the movements into a dramatic context by taking the children on an imaginary journey in which the spacial concepts feature strongly. An example is given below.

Imagine that you're walking on the bottom of the sea. It's hard work pushing against all that water, so you'll go slowly. The water is all around you. Use your arms to feel the water everywhere. Stop now, because there's something big above you. It's a huge whale swimming over your head. Point to it. The whale is coming to see you. It's right behind you. Turn around to face it. Now the whale is in front of you. Look out! It's throwing you up onto its back! Sit down on the whale's back. Now the whale is below you. Point to it. The whale is taking you on a journey and all sorts of interesting things are whizzing by. If I ask you, tell me what you can see. Is it a giant fish? Or a shipwreck? Or an octopus? *(Ask some of the children to tell everyone what they see.)* Now the whale is putting you down near a door. Is the door in front of you? above you? below you? behind you, or beside you? *(Ask some of the children for answers.)* I expect the door is quite stiff and hard to open. Show how you open it. I wonder what's inside the door. Go in and have a look.

Now sit down on the floor while some of you tell the rest of us what you found behind your door under the sea. *(Ask for responses.)*

---

100 Scale

Drama space
Classroom or hall

Other subject link
Geography

Organisation
Pairs or individuals, small groups

Age
7–9

Purpose
● To introduce the idea of scale.

Activities
1 Talk about the idea of a shrinking machine, which can reduce a child to the size of an ant. The film, *Honey I Shrunk the Kids*, might be a good example to draw on or even show a clip from. Another way of introducing the theme would be through Micro machines, the popular scaled down toys.

2 In pairs or individually, the children draw their own designs for a shrinking machine.

3 Choose a spot in the classroom or a desktop which would present a number of challenges to an ant. Gather round and examine the area closely. Ask the class to imagine what it would look like from the perspective of an ant. Encourage them to think about details such as specks of dust, carpet pile or hairs, desk legs, and so on. What would be the major obstacles? What things would an ant ignore? What would it climb over? What would it go round?

4 In small groups, the children enact the journey across the given area. Encourage them to think about how the change in scale of everyday objects affects them, not only by size but also by weight and action. For example, a hot air blower might be very hard to walk past and an open window presents all sorts of dangers. Allow them to talk about their experiences as they move.

5 If appropriate, some groups could enact their journey for the rest of the class.

Further activities
► Ask the children to write or tell their own stories about how they were shrunk.
► Encourage descriptive writing, poems and artwork on the theme of scale.
► Use this work as a springboard for maths work on the theme.

dog

bat

hit

let

The drought of Chi-Min-Tin

The village of Chi-Min-Tin was very hot and dry. It hadn't rained for many months and the land was brown and dusty. All the flowers had died and even the leaves on the trees were shrivelling and falling to the earth. The animals were sick and the village well had almost dried up. Something had to be done.

Each day at sunrise the villagers prayed to the gods for rain. They danced and sang and clapped their hands to please the rain gods but no rain fell. Only clear blue skies and the sun hotter than ever. The village elder called a meeting. He did not speak but scratched a pattern in the dusty earth with a long thin stick. It was a pattern with pointed triangles. It represented the Jagyard mountains. All the older villagers nodded their heads. The elder lifted the stick and started to swing it round his head. Faster and faster it swung, then stopped suddenly and pointed straight at Mi-Lin. This young girl was the chosen one. Her task was to climb high into the Jagyard mountains to try and meet the rain gods. She could choose one companion to go with her.

By village law, no one could speak to Mi-Lin as she left. They turned their backs as the two set out with just a day's supply of water between them. All the villagers worried silently as the girls' absence turned into two days.

Just before nightfall of the third day, the two tiny figures walked very slowly and shakily into the village. The gods had spoken, ordering that all things made of metal were to be buried deep in the ground. Then and only then would there be rain. The villagers peered at the two exhausted travellers wondering if they heard correctly.

The elder started drawing. He scratched out a big circle on the brown earth and one villager came running with a spade. By the flicker of firelight, a circular pit was dug. Everyone brought their metal objects to be buried. The rains came before sunrise in torrents. The village rejoiced and gave thanks to the gods with a special song. Tiny plants burst from the brown earth with flowers of red and orange.

Still the rain came and each day it was heavier. There was an end to the song of thanks.

The roots of the tiny plants were washed away and a great wind sprang up. Houses were blown down and the villagers knew the gods were angry again.

The elder again called a meeting and asked the villagers in turn if they could think why the gods were angry. No one offered a reason. The elder pointed his stick at Mi-Lin. She chose a companion and once more set out to speak to the gods.

Mi-Lin and her companion had taken but three steps out of the village when there was a mighty thunderbolt from the sky. Vast showers of metal fell. Shiny car wheels, gears, mirrors, number plates, bumpers, doors, axles, pipes and metal sheets thudded down in a great heap in the middle of the village. An eerie silence followed. Many people had run into their houses to escape the falling objects. Others stood transfixed. A sound of crying and wailing broke through the silence.

'It is I,' cried Chen, 'I who have angered the gods. I dug these things out of the pit. In the secret of night I took them and made myself a motor car.'

When every last piece of metal was once again buried deep in the pit, the rains ended. Happiness came once more to the village of Chi-Min-Tin. It was a happiness that lasted. It was happiness without metal and cars.

100 ideas for Drama ©HarperCollins*Publishers* 1997

Robin Hood's Bullseye

The market square in Nottingham at the time of Robin Hood. People are buying and selling food, cloth and other goods. There are jugglers and other entertainers. Overlooking all is the Sheriff of Nottingham. To one side, near a group of soldiers, a large archery target is being set up. One of the soldiers steps forward and reads from a scroll.

Soldier 1: Today is the Sheriff's archery contest. Any person of Nottingham can try their skill. Be ready, people of Nottingham. Step forward.

The crowd all step back. Nobody wants to enter the contest. They all fear the Sheriff.

Soldier 2: Come, good people. The prize is a silver arrow. Whoever hits the centre of the target will be the winner.

Soldier 3: Come, now. The Sheriff himself has called this contest.

There is silence. The Sheriff and the soldiers look into the crowd. A figure in a cloak steps forward.

Robin: I will try.

Soldier 1: Oh, will you?

Robin: I will.

Soldier 2: Are you a man of Nottingham?

Robin: I am.

Sheriff: Let him shoot.

Soldier 3: Step up to the mark.

Robin steps forward and is given a bow and arrow. He tests the bow, pulling back the string. All this is done in mime.

Robin: This is poor tackle. It's all twisted. No one could hit a tree trunk at two paces with this.

Sheriff: Another bow! Bring this bold fellow another bow.

Another bow is brought and Robin mimes pulling the string all the way back to his ear. It is hard to pull it so far.

Sheriff: Where did you learn to draw the bow like that?

Robin: I learned it from Robin Hood, Sir.

Sheriff: You know this Robin Hood, do you?

Robin: I must have shot with him a hundred times in Sherwood Forest.

Sheriff: He is an outlaw, and when I have him in my hands ...

Robin: If you're a little patient, Sir, I believe it will not be long before you see Robin Hood face to face.

Robin mimes shooting his arrow. It hits the centre of the target. The crowd cheers.

Soldier 1: Dead middle. Bull's eye.

Sheriff: Bull's eye indeed!

Robin: The silver arrow is mine, I believe.

Sheriff: Of course.

The sheriff approaches to shake Robin by the hand. He suddenly pulls back the hood of Robin's cloak.

Sheriff: But the prize is mine!

The soldiers quickly surround Robin. One takes his bow and the others hold him firmly.

Sheriff: So, our fine marksman is none other than Robin Hood himself. Take him to Nottingham castle for the night. At dawn tomorrow he hangs.

My magical journey

Imagine that you are going to the shops with a grown up,
but today everything has become magical.

► **Fill in the spaces in this story.
Make it as exciting and magical as you can.**

This morning I went shopping with _____ .

We went into the bakery. I peeped into the oven and I saw

_____ .

Then we went to the greengrocers. I had a bite of a big red apple

and suddenly _____

_____

_____ .

In a cage in the pet shop there was a _____ .

I watched it and it _____ .

In the supermarket I rode in a _____ .

On the shelves were hundreds of _____ .

Just as we were going outside I saw a huge _____

_____ .

Then I _____

_____

_____ .

100 ideas for Drama ©HarperCollins*Publishers* 1997

It was very dark as we travelled by horse and coach, ever closer to the castle. And it was cold, so very cold. A cold that bites. The land and sky seemed to merge into one dark mist. There was gloom about the trees and our bumpy roadway was like a tunnel beneath the overhanging branches. The baying of wolves sounded nearer, ever nearer, as though the animals were closing in on us from every side.

I had given up hope of ever seeing light again when, suddenly, to our left I saw a faint, flickering, blue flame. What little comfort I took from this light was soon exhausted as the coach driver pulled hard on the reins. The horse reared and snorted in terror. The coach ground to a halt. All was quiet except for the wolves who now seemed close enough to touch!

'This is as far as I go,' said the coachman.
'But...'
'Over yonder is the Count's castle. You must walk now.'

I peered into the gloom and saw an iron gate in front of the huge, forbidding stone wall of the castle. Reluctantly I climbed down from the coach and took three steps towards the gate. Turning to bid farewell to the coachman, I could see nothing of its form. Coach, horse, driver – all had disappeared into thin air.

DRAFT SCRIPT — HOLDING THE BABY

WRITTEN BY ALEX COOGAN — PAGE 8

The bedroom of Jim and Karen. The two are arguing.

>JIM
>You didn't tell me it was today.

>KAREN
>Tell you! ... Tell you! Of course I told you. I told you all about it over a month ago. Only...

>JIM
>Only what?

>KAREN
>Only you weren't listening. Jim, I'm not arguing about it. I'm late as it is. You'll manage. It's only a couple of days. I'll be back on Tuesday.

>JIM
>Tuesday! How do you mean, Tuesday?

>KAREN
>Look, I've got to go. I've explained everything loads of times. You know where everything is. Bye...

>JIM
>But...

Karen leaves.

Cut to Jim looking out of window as Karen disappears.

Cut to double carrycot on the table.

Jim takes a few steps towards it and peeks in.

He tiptoes away again and sits down to read his newspaper.

Every so often he looks up towards the carrycot.

After a while a baby gurgles.

Jim ducks quickly behind his paper.

His expression shows he is determined to ignore the babies.

More baby sounds.

Jim looks reluctantly at the carrycot.

A baby's hand appears playing with a rattle.

The rattle bangs against the edge of the carrycot.

Then it is flung down into the carrycot. The other baby screams.

>JIM
>Oh! No!

Both babies cry loudly. Jim holds his head in his hands.

100 ideas for Drama ©HarperCollins*Publishers* 1997

A midsummer night's dream:

Puck's tricks

Section 1

I jest to Oberon,

and make him smile,

When I a fat

and bean-fed horse beguile,

Neighing in likeness

of a filly foal:

Section 2

And sometimes lurk I

in a gossip's bowl,

In very likeness

of a roasted crab;

And, when she drinks,

against her lips, I bob,

And on her wither'd dew-lap

pour the ale.

Section 3

The wisest aunt,

telling the saddest tale,

Sometimes for three-foot stool

mistaketh me;

Then slip I from her bum,

down topples she.

Romeo and Juliet:
The hatred of the Montagues and Capulets

In Verona, a city in Italy, there lived two families who hated each other and were always arguing and fighting. One family, the Capulets, had a daughter called Juliet. The other family, the Montagues, had a son called Romeo.

Juliet's parents had arranged for her to marry a handsome young nobleman called Paris. They decided to throw a big party to give Juliet and Paris a chance to get to know each other. Romeo, his cousin, Benvolio, and their friend, Mercutio, decided to gate crash. They wore masks so that no one would know them. Juliet's cousin, Tybalt, recognised Romeo and wanted to throw him and his companions out, but Juliet's father didn't want any trouble.

Romeo and Juliet meet at the party
Romeo and Juliet met for the first time at the party and fell in love with each other straightaway. After the party, Romeo waited in the garden and Juliet talked to him from her balcony. Juliet discovered that Romeo was a Montague but she didn't care.

Romeo and Juliet marry in secret
The next day Juliet sent her nurse to find Romeo. The nurse brought back a note from Romeo which said that he would marry Juliet in secret the day after. A priest called Friar Laurence married them. They couldn't tell their parents, who were sworn enemies.

Romeo kills Juliet's cousin, Tybalt, and is banished
Later that day Romeo and Mercutio met Tybalt. Tybalt wanted to fight but Romeo tried to make friends with him. Mercutio, thinking Romeo was a coward, started to fight Tybalt. Romeo tried to break it up and, in the scuffle, Tybalt killed Mercutio. Romeo, in anger, killed Tybalt. Before he died, Mercutio put a curse on both families. When the crimes were discovered, Romeo was banished by the ruler, the Prince of Verona.

Juliet hears the news
When Juliet heard the news, she didn't know which was worse, Tybalt's death or Romeo's banishment. But she realised she was crying for Romeo. Her parents, who knew nothing of her marriage to Romeo, thought she was upset over her cousin's death. They decided that she should marry Paris quickly to cheer her up.

Friar Laurence gives Juliet a sleeping potion
Juliet didn't know what to do. She went to see Friar Laurence and threatened to kill herself if he didn't help her. He came up with a plan. He gave her a sleeping potion which would make her look as though she were dead. Juliet took the potion and everyone thought she had died. She was taken to the family tomb. The friar sent a message to Romeo to come and take Juliet away, as planned, but the messenger was delayed and the news of Juliet's death reached Romeo first.

The deaths of Romeo and Juliet
Romeo bought a bottle of poison and came to the tomb where he met Paris, who started a fight. Romeo killed Paris. Then he took the poison and died at Juliet's side. When Juliet woke up and found Romeo dead, she killed herself with his dagger. When the bodies were discovered, only Friar Laurence could explain what had happened. The two families realised that their hatred had killed their children. They vowed to fight no more.

Who's who in Romeo and Juliet

Capulet Family	Montague Family	Others
Juliet	Romeo	The Prince – *ruler of Verona*
Juliet's father	Romeo's father	Mercutio – *relation of the Prince and Romeo's friend*
Juliet's mother		
Tybalt – *Juliet's cousin*	Romeo's mother	
Juliet's nurse	Benvolio – *Romeo's cousin*	Paris – *relation of the Prince and engaged to Juliet*
		Friar Laurence – *a priest*

100 ideas for Drama ©HarperCollins*Publishers* 1997

The worst report ever

Create a play script from the following section of a story.

▶ **Follow these steps:**

1 Highlight in two different colours what each character says.

2 Highlight in a third colour any description of the setting (where the action takes place).

3 Highlight in a fourth colour any description of the actions (what the characters do).

4 Start your play version with the setting and stage directions for the actor. (Ask your teacher for a copy of pcm 19, 24 or 54 to get started.)

5 Continue with dialogue and stage directions to the end of the scene. (Take the dialogue from the story. You can change the words, but do not change the meaning.)

6 Look at the version your teacher has. Do you like hers better?

'I knew this was it,' Lee thought. His mother was coming in. There was the report on the table where he'd left it. 'Oh, man, she's going to kill me. It isn't just a bad report. It's the worst report in the school! Ever!'

The front door closed. Lee's mum was walking towards the kitchen. 'Now,' he said to himself. 'Now it's going to happen.' Before he could stop himself, his hand shot out and picked up the brown envelope. 'I can't let Mum see it. I can't.'

She was just outside the kitchen. It was in his hand. 'What can I do with it?! he thought frantically. The door was opening. He couldn't think. He stood up. 'Hello, Lee,' said Mum. She hadn't seen it yet, so he hurriedly put the report on the chair and sat down again quickly.

'Good day, love?'

'Yeah, fine, Mum.' His voice sounded terrible, like he had swallowed the report. Next minute he wished he had.

'Make me a cup of tea will you, Lee?

I'm tired out.'

To make a cup of tea he'd have to get up. If he got up she'd see the brown envelope. He had to think fast.

'Come on, love. I'm really tired. Please make the tea while I put the shopping away.'

'Well, you see, Mum,' he started to say. He needed to think fast, but he couldn't think at all.

Luckily, just at that moment, he heard the sweetest, most brilliant sound in the world. The phone rang and his mother went to answer it.

As soon as she left the room, he shoved the envelope in his pocket, and not a moment too soon because his mum was back in the room in seconds. She looked very upset.

'Lee,' she said, and something in the tone of her voice told him what was coming. 'That was your teacher, Lee. She asked if I'd had a chance to look at your report yet. She thinks I'll be concerned. Where is it?'

I know what you're thinking

Granny comes in with a birthday present for Jenny.

FREEZE: Jenny speaks her thoughts:
'I hope it's sweets or money'.

SCENE CONTINUES: Jenny opens the present.
It's a handkerchief. She says, 'It's lovely!'

FREEZE: Granny speaks her thoughts:
'I knew she'd like it'.

SCENE ENDS: Granny and Jenny say good-bye.

Daleville Primary School
The Vale
Daleville
D6 0S

Tel: 01111 987654

Dear Mrs Simpson

I am writing to ask if you would come and see me sometime this week. Joe's teacher and I are both concerned about his behaviour and we wanted to discuss this with you.

Please call Miss James, the school secretary, to arrange an appointment.

I look forward to meeting you.

Yours sincerely,

G Mitchell

Headteacher

Laura's story

We were playing and it just broke. Crash went the window. Smash went the glass everywhere. All by itself… smash. I never did anything. Really I didn't.

Ben, that's my older brother, says we shouldn't say anything about the bat and ball. He says it was my fault anyway, for not catching the ball. Ben says Mum will tell us off proper when she sees it. 'It's best to say it wasn't us,' he said. 'Yes,' I said back to him. 'It wasn't us.' Only thing is, Mum says always tell the truth… always… always. But I don't want to be told off and, anyway, I didn't do it. Really… really… really…

Football for girls

I can't believe it. I went up to her house as usual on Saturday and she was out. 'Didn't you know?' said her dad. 'She's gone to football.' I didn't know anything about it. I didn't know she liked watching football or what team she supported. But I got it wrong. She isn't watching football, she's playing it. She's joined an all girl's team. Would you believe it? And what's worse, this team are top of the league… beating all the boys' teams flat.

When I saw her on Monday, she said she hadn't said anything about it because I'd only laugh at her. She's hoping to get a regular place in the team and play every Saturday and go to training on Sundays. I was gutted… anyway, football's a man's game… always has been and always will be. That's what my dad says and I reckon he's right.

Dear David,
I don't want to be your
friend any more so
please stop hanging
around me at breaktime.
With this letter are the
two books you lent me.
Please don't ask me why,
you know why.
M.

Nobody likes me!

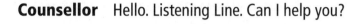

Counsellor	Hello. Listening Line. Can I help you?
Sam	I hope so.
Counsellor	So do I. My name's Jenny. What's yours?
Sam	Sam.
Counsellor	And what's the problem, Sam?
Sam	Well, it's just that I feel really lonely. I don't have any friends and nobody likes me.
Counsellor	Has something happened recently to make you feel like this?
Sam	Yes. Rebecca used to be my best friend and today in the playground she said that Alice is her best friend and she doesn't want to play with me anymore…

Toni is 9 years old and has just smoked her first cigarette.

I did it. Today I had my first fag. Sean passed it to me and said, 'Go on, have a go. It won't hurt you.' So I did. Closed my eyes, took a deep breath and that was that. I had a smoke. I did cough a bit. Maybe the breath was too deep but I managed. Don't know what all the fuss is about. My mother going on about smoking all the time and how she wished she'd never started. It's just a laugh really. I mean one fag… it's not as if I'm addicted, is it?

100 ideas for Drama ©HarperCollins*Publishers* 1997

Jo is at a party after school with three great friends, Kirsty, Dave and Alex. They've been dancing non-stop and are worn out. They sit down to have a rest. Alex disappears and comes back with a can of beer and offers it around. Kirsty giggles and takes a swig. Dave refuses at first but Alex persuades him to have some. Jo is the only one who won't have a drink. The others call her chicken and put pressure on her to drink. Jo becomes aware that others are looking at her. She doesn't want to look like a prude but, at the same time, she knows that none of them should be drinking.

100 ideas for Drama © HarperCollins*Publishers* 1997

Odd one out

Peter and his Mum are having tea

Peter Oh, yeah, Mum. There's a letter for you. From school.

Mum I'll have a look after tea.

Peter It's okay. I'll get it now.

Peter rushes off to get the letter out of his backpack

Mum What's all the rush? Sit down and finish your tea.

Peter It's okay. Here it is.

Peter sits down with the letter and gives it to his Mum

Mum *(Reads)* Oh, I see.

Peter Can I go, Mum? Please?

Mum It's a lot of money, Peter. One hundred and twenty pounds. I don't think…

Peter It is a whole week, Mum, and the whole class is going.

Mum But where will the money come from?

Peter You always say that. I want to go, everyone else is.

Mum Everyone else, Peter?

Peter All my friends are going. I don't want to be left out.

Mum I'm just saying...

Peter Come on, Mum.

Mum *(Thinks carefully)* I'm sorry, Peter. I know how much you want to go on the school journey but I just don't think…

Peter It's always the same, always. Why can't we be like everyone else? Why do I always have to be the odd one out?

Mum Peter, listen to me…

Peter I'm not listening. I'm going.

Peter storms out leaving his Mum alone at the table. She picks up the letter and reads it again, shaking her head as she does so.

Head shaved

Karlo is 12 years old. He has just had his head shaved to spell 'Addid'.

We seen this thing on the telly, about shaving your head with a logo. And Brooko, one of my mates, says, 'That's for us, Karlo.'

'Why not?' says Fluella. So we done it.

We got Brooko's dad's electric shaver and had a go. Nobody wanted to try it at first, so Fluella showed us how. She's sharp. She made this really good shape of Brooko's head. She's an artist. Even her teacher says she's good at art.

Then it was my go. I wanted really big letters on my head, and no picture. Trouble was, the letters were too big, and she ran out of space before she could do all the word. So I got ADDID. I didn't mind. It was a bit of a laugh, really. Except next day at school, they sent me home. Said I couldn't go to school looking like that. What do they expect me to do about it?

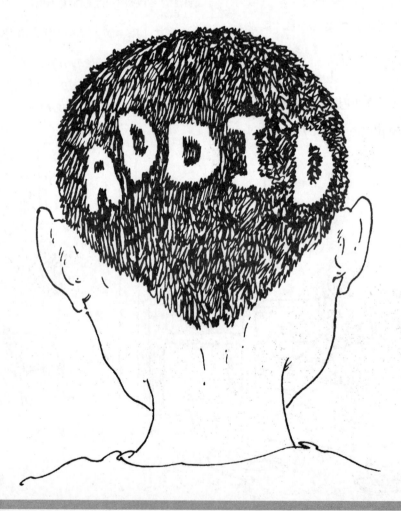

100 ideas for Drama ©HarperCollins*Publishers* 1997

Victorian childhood

The Chimney Sweep

'We get up very early, while it's still dark. If we're lucky, we get a piece of bread for breakfast. Then we all set off for the first house. Sometimes we have to walk very far but you have to keep up or the master will wallop you.

I'm used to it now, but the first time I went up the chimney I was so scared. You have to crawl up in the dark and try to find holes for your hands and feet. I tried to come back down but the master said he'd start a fire under me to make me go up. When I started to brush the soot down, it all went in my mouth. I could hardly breathe. When I got down my arms and knees were bleeding. One of the other boys rubbed salt into the cuts. I screamed but it made my skin much tougher.

Once one of the sweeps fell and broke his leg. I never saw him again.'

In the factory

'My job is to clean the machines in the lace factory. I have to crawl underneath the machines and pull out bits of thread that have got caught up. I have to do it when the machines are going. The noise is horrible and I'm terrified that I'll get my hair caught. That happened to one girl and she was killed. It was horrible. My back is getting quite bent because I spend so much time bending over. I've seen people who can't straighten up at all. I'm really scared that will happen to me.'

Down the mine

'Sundays are the only time I see daylight. I work as a trapper. That means I have to stay all day in the dark and open and shut the trap door for the coal to be brought through. Sometimes I'm really frightened in the dark. The day's so long it's hard to stay awake, but if you fall asleep a coal truck might run over your legs. All my family works in the mines. My older brother used to haul coal trucks. He was 10 years old. One day there was an accident and he got buried under a fall of coal. By the time they found him, he was dead. I miss him.'

School life

'Some people would say I'm lucky because my parents can afford to send me to school, but I don't think so. The school is very cold and dingy and we're always hungry. The lessons are hard, and if we don't know an answer straight off, we get beaten. One of my friends was beaten just because his parents were late with his fees. But even worse than the beatings is the caster oil. It's thick and tastes disgusting. We have to swallow a spoonful every morning and someone is always sick afterwards.

The older boys are as bad as the masters. They make us work for them, and if we don't please them, they beat us.'

100 ideas for Drama ©HarperCollins*Publishers* 1997

The blitz

It was the morning of May 5th. I was on my way to work when our bus was stopped by the police who said that both roads into town were closed. We were told that part of the town had been wiped out by incendiary and high explosive bombs and that there was still danger of unexploded bombs.

Some of us walked into what was left of the town. As we got closer, we could see smoke and rubble ahead.

We had to wet handkerchiefs in the river to hold over our mouths and noses as we ran through the smoking remains of a factory. We passed a pile of stones that once had been a cottage and a small shop. When we reached the place where we once worked, we were horrified to see that the shipyard, store and office block had been completely destroyed. Charred timbers and twisted metal was all that was left.

When the Railway came

Railway opponents

WE THE UNDERSIGNED,

Landowners, Clergy, Yeoman, Traders and other Inhabitants, have seen with extreme surprise ADVERTISEMENTS for a project for establishing RAILWAYS in our County.

We hereby declare our direct and determined HOSTILITY to this WILD and DANGEROUS speculation, which, so far from benefiting our County, would PAINFULLY affect its interests, and would THREATEN with RUIN its inhabitants.

We do not require any facilities of transport other than those which we presently enjoy. We cannot believe that any living person would wish to exchange the quiet enjoyment of pleasure and health for the HORRID SPEED of the Railway.

We do, therefore, PROTEST most anxiously and earnestly against a proposal thrust upon us contrary to our wishes, involving serious RISK to the speculators, threatening deep INJURY through Railway ACCIDENTS, and being utterly useless and valueless to the community at large.

Railway supporters

A GOLDEN OPPORTUNITY

Friends,

A new age is upon us. A new age of golden opportunity. It is, friends, the time of the Railway whose great iron hands reach out to embrace us all… whose very fingertips, in this, the civilised spirit of our age, reaches out to touch every business locality and fashionable neighbourhood in the British Isles. Such parts as remain without this great iron strength will suffer serious and sustained decline and hardship.

Many great towns shall be as one; friends residing at a distance will more frequently visit; the interchange of thought and feeling will enlarge understanding. Tourists and Invalids will more easily enjoy our beautiful scenery and our climate. Coals in our town will cost some 22s a ton instead of 35s a ton as at present.

Friends, do not delay for one moment. Shares in this great venture are available now for £10. A mere one guinea is sufficient for a deposit. Who will be the first?

THE RAILWAY COMPANY

Fact Sheet

Thomas More

When did Thomas More live?
He lived in the reign of King Henry VIII over 400 years ago. When Henry was crowned, Thomas wrote: 'This day is the end of slavery, the fount of our liberty: the end of sadness, the beginning of joy.'

Why is Thomas More famous?
Because he defied Henry VIII and died for his beliefs. Henry broke with the church of Rome and declared himself head of the English church. He did this so he could divorce his wife, which the Pope would not allow. Thomas would not support Henry's action. He believed the Pope to be the church's true head and he opposed the divorce.

What did King Henry do?
He put Thomas in prison and put pressure on him to change his mind. He only allowed Thomas' family to visit him in prison so that they could try to persuade him to accept Henry as head of the church.

Did Thomas change his mind?
No. Thomas stood by his beliefs, saying his duty to God always came first. After a year in prison, he was executed. His final words were: 'I die loyal to God and the King, but to God first of all.'

Where can I find out more about Thomas More?
In history books dealing with Henry VIII. 'A Man for All Seasons' by Robert Bolt is a powerful play and film about More's life.

Wreckers

The life of the wreckers

We live close to starvation. When the weather is good we can fish. When the weather is bad, as it often is round here, we cannot fish. In the winter that can be week after week. The land will not support crops so we have nothing if we cannot fish. It is the children we fear most for, and families are big. So when a ship comes adrift on the rocks, times are good for a while. We've seen French brandy, purest silk in bales, jewels, boxes of the finest food you could ever wish to see come from the wrecks. Most times the things come ashore down in the cove for anyone to carry away. Then it's our harvest time for sure. That's the only time we take stuff from the wrecks and the only time there's a smile on our faces.

The viewpoint of a
Customs and Excise Officer

These wreckers are desperate people who lure innocent ships ashore by placing lights on dangerous rocks. Year after year ships come to grief believing the lights to be those of a safe harbour, only to be dashed to pieces on treacherous rocks. These people are more evil than the sea itself and they must be stopped. Any person causing a shipwreck should be hung!

100 ideas for Drama © HarperCollins*Publishers* 1997

Mrs B. Watson

103 Phibbs Street

London E11

Dear Mum and Dad
Arrived safely. We were all
tired but we had to stand
in line and wait for people
to choose us. It was
horrible. Mrs Lewis picked
me. She's nice but she
talks funny and sometimes
I can't understand her.
Rose is my age. She says
I don't talk right and
makes fun of me. There's
lots more food here. We
had eggs for tea. I miss
you very much. I hope I
can come home soon.
Lots of love Jean

IDENTITY CARD

Surname of family

First name of person travelling

Age

Job (if adult)

Place travelling from

Year of journey

Month of journey

Picture of person (draw yourself)

OFFICIAL

100 ideas for Drama © HarperCollins*Publishers* 1997

An Icelandic legend

At the dawn of time, say the ancient storytellers of Iceland, there was neither land or icy waves. The earth did not exist, nor the sky over it. Nowhere did grass grow. There was to the north a huge cave, a world of clouds and shadows. Suddenly, in the middle of the huge cave, a magnificent fountain burst forth. From this fountain began to flow the icy waters of twelve rivers.

To the south lay the land of fire. From there poured rivers of poison and fire, which little by little set and became solid. When the ice from the north met the fire from the south, there came the first coatings of white frost. When the fire from the south met the ice rivers from the north, warm air blew and the ice began to melt. From the very first melting drops was formed Yamir, a giant with a human-like body. He was the first of all living things. In his sleep he gave birth to a man and a woman from under his left arm. They grew to be giants like him.

From the sparks of Yamir's eyes, the gods made the sun, moon and countless stars. From his bones the gods made mountains and from his hair, the trees. The sun, travelling across the southern sky, threw its light and warmth over vast stretches of the earth. Soon appeared the first blades of grass.

A Native American myth

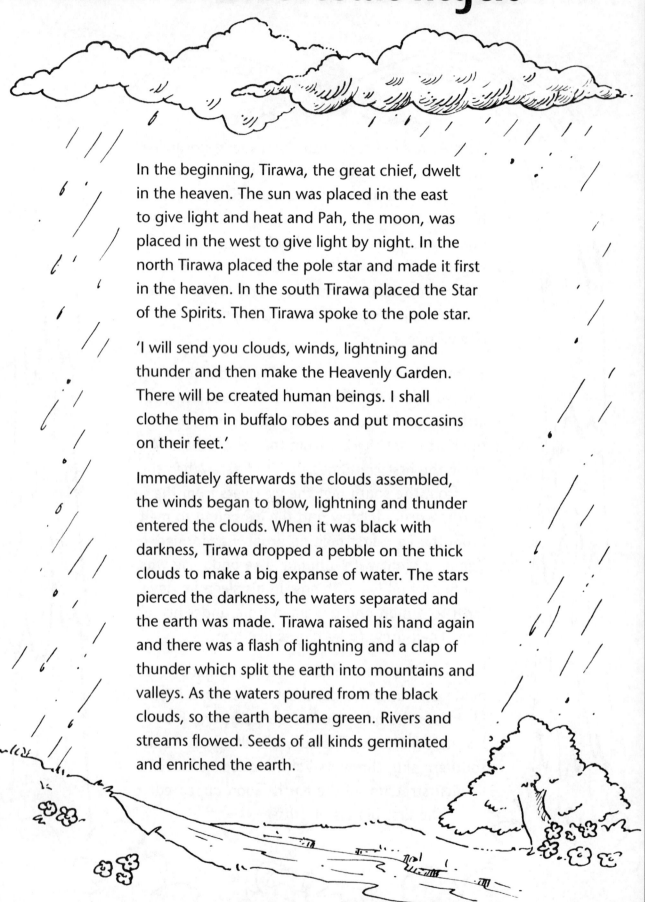

In the beginning, Tirawa, the great chief, dwelt in the heaven. The sun was placed in the east to give light and heat and Pah, the moon, was placed in the west to give light by night. In the north Tirawa placed the pole star and made it first in the heaven. In the south Tirawa placed the Star of the Spirits. Then Tirawa spoke to the pole star.

'I will send you clouds, winds, lightning and thunder and then make the Heavenly Garden. There will be created human beings. I shall clothe them in buffalo robes and put moccasins on their feet.'

Immediately afterwards the clouds assembled, the winds began to blow, lightning and thunder entered the clouds. When it was black with darkness, Tirawa dropped a pebble on the thick clouds to make a big expanse of water. The stars pierced the darkness, the waters separated and the earth was made. Tirawa raised his hand again and there was a flash of lightning and a clap of thunder which split the earth into mountains and valleys. As the waters poured from the black clouds, so the earth became green. Rivers and streams flowed. Seeds of all kinds germinated and enriched the earth.

100 ideas for Drama ©HarperCollins*Publishers* 1997

The Trimurti

Hindu people have many different stories about the creation of the world. One version comes from the ancient writings called the Veda. It says that the world has been made and destroyed many times before and that this will happen again.

Brahma

**Vishnu
(in his human form as Rama)**

Shiva

The Trimurti are the three parts of the one Supreme Spirit of Hindu belief. Of the three parts, Brahma creates the universe and all life. Vishnu protects and preserves life. Shiva destroys people and things.

As the creator, Brahma makes the world. Everything from the largest animal to the smallest insect comes out of Brahma's body. When Brahma has finished his work, he goes to sleep.

A day for Brahma lasts millions of years. While he sleeps, Vishnu looks after the world. When the world grows too old, Shiva destroys what is aged and useless, but allows new things to happen. When Brahma wakes, he makes the world again.

To Leisure Centre, 1km

School

**Shopping
Centre**

Remains of old Roman Wall

Waste ground

100 ideas for Drama ©HarperCollins*Publishers* 1997

Is a dog a person's best friend?

Please tick a Yes or No box for each question.

Make up some questions of your own for **5**, **6**, **7** and **8**.

1 Do you have a dog?

Yes ☐   No ☐

2 Do you like dogs?

Yes ☐   No ☐

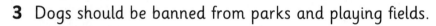

3 Dogs should be banned from parks and playing fields.

Agree ☐   Disagree ☐   Not sure ☐

4 People should only be allowed to have one dog.

Agree ☐   Disagree ☐   Not sure ☐

5 _____

Agree ☐   Disagree ☐   Not sure ☐

6 _____

Agree ☐   Disagree ☐   Not sure ☐

7 _____

Agree ☐   Disagree ☐   Not sure ☐

8 _____

Agree ☐   Disagree ☐   Not sure ☐

Ideas to save the environment

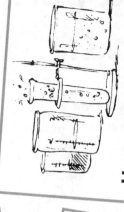

Walk more or take public transportation if your family uses a car. Find out how cars pollute the air

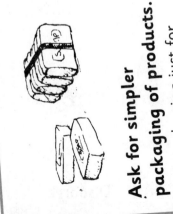

Use products that have been designed not to harm the environment. Find out about 'environmental friendly' products and the shops that sell them

Repair and reuse toys and clothing. Think about swapping useable things you're tired of or have outgrown

Explore alternative forms of energy. Wind, water and solar energies are already in use

Recycle paper and card, bottles and tins. Find out how you can raise money for your school by recycling

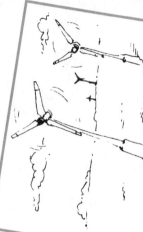

Plant vegetable gardens, flowers and trees. Find out how vegetation helps the planet

Use less electricity and gas at home and school. Think about heating, lighting, cooking

Ask for simpler packaging of products. Overpackaging just for looks uses up lots of paper and plastic

100 ideas for Drama ©*HarperCollinsPublishers* 1997